FAME

CLIVE JAMES

FAME

IN THE 20th CENTURY

RANDOM HOUSE
NEW YORK

FAME IS THE SUM TOTAL OF ALL

THE MISUNDERSTANDINGS

THAT CAN GATHER

AROUND ONE NAME.

RAINER MARIA RILKE, 1875-1926

All rights reserved under International and Pan-American Copyright Conventions.
Published in the United States by Random House, Inc., New York.

This work was originally published in Great Britain by BBC Books, a division of
BBC Enterprises Limited, London.

Library of Congress Cataloging-in-Publication Data

James, Clive
Fame in the 20th century / Clive James.
p.   cm.
Includes index.
ISBN 0-679-42699-X
1. Biography—20th century.   2. Celebrities—Biography.
3. Success—History.   4. Success—Humor.   5. Fame—Humor.
I. Title.   II. Title: Fame in the twentieth century.
CT120.J35   1993
920′.009′04—dc20   93-4180

Manufactured in the United States of America
2   4   6   8   9   7   5   3
First U.S. Edition

Designed by Harry Green
Set in Garamond Simoncini
Filmset by Selwood Systems, Midsomer Norton, England
Color separation by Technik Limited, Berkhamsted, England

CONTENTS

TO

RICHARD DREWETT

INTRODUCTION

Not all books are collaborations, although some are. All television programmes are collaborations without exception. So there is no use my writing an introduction to this book – essentially the book of the series – as if it were all my own work. The book wouldn't exist without the series and the series wouldn't exist without its Producer, Beatrice Ballard. *Fame in the Twentieth Century* started as an idea by her. It took her three years of fanatically dedicated work, supervising every detail of its immense effort in scripting, research, editing and administration, to make the idea a reality. You have to imagine a whole corridor lined with cutting rooms full of editors toiling like troglodytes; another corridor lined with viewing rooms manned by red-eyed researchers working a two-shift system; a block-long open plan office full of sweating personnel hunched at word processors – and this mere slip of a woman controlling it all with a smile here, a quiet word there, and only the occasional flourish of her fifteen-foot Australian stock whip. Watching her in action through the slit in my cell door, I was able to remind myself that my part was the easy part, even when it didn't feel like it.

Actually it never felt like it. From my angle the whole deal, from the very first meeting, had the same leisure opportunities as a life sentence in the engine room of a trireme. It took a dozen of us almost all of the first week to agree on the 250 twentieth-century people who were genuinely, undeniably world-famous. Placido Domingo was out because his name was known only to everyone on Earth who liked the sound of good singing. Luciano Pavarotti was known even to people who couldn't tell good singing from bad, so he was in. Picasso was in and Matisse was out. Stefan Edberg was out because you had to be interested in tennis. John McEnroe was in because everybody was interested in bad behaviour. Those who were in got a blue card each so they could be pinned to the wall. It was incredible, the magnitude of some of the names that didn't get on that wall. When I realized that Margaret Mitchell was going to rate a mention but T. S. Eliot wasn't I argued for a pink card category for people who should get a *fleeting* mention. Pink cards joined the blue cards. When the wall looked like a tennis court painted by Piet Mondrian, I was led away, locked up in my office and told to come out when I had a rough draft of the script.

It took two years. We were doing other programmes as well, of course, but every minute I didn't spend on them I spent driving myself nuts trying to crack the format of *Fame*. I was determined to make the narrative chronological. When I first studied history at Sydney University in the late 1950s, a big debate was going on about whether individual personalities had any effect on the flow of events. My own belief, then as now, was that nothing else did. History is just the sum total of what personalities do. The complication arises from the awkward fact that absolutely everybody's personality counts, anonymous people included. But to deny that famous people influence events is essentially fatuous. Of course they do. A history of the twentieth century without Hitler, Stalin, Mussolini, Mao, Churchill, Roosevelt, Einstein – no matter how full of sociological jargon, it would be hopelessly empty. Conversely, to talk about the famous people of the twentieth century must be to talk about its history. By now, having lived a full half of that century myself, I had my own interpretation of what had been going on. On the first day of writing the script I sketched an outline of what I took to be the big story of modern times – the long conflict between democracy and totalitarianism. My main task would be to unfold that narrative while simultaneously reflecting on the biographies of the leading characters, and doing all that while simultaneously reflecting on the development of the means of communication that made fame increasingly pervasive, and doing all that while simultaneously reflecting on how the condition of actually being famous changed with circumstances, and doing all that while simultaneously specifying how everything I mentioned might be illustrated with footage, stills, posters and choice quotations read out by myself in a flatteringly lit mid-shot.

After writing twenty-two separate drafts of Episode One I was a cot-case being fed through a vein. Months had gone by and the office and the corridors were waist-deep with teetering stacks of film cans and videotapes loaded with off-line edits of famous people doing famous things. Everyone gathered around my bed while we faced reality. We had learned the hard way that we were dealing with a whole new type of television series. It was an enormous three-dimensional jigsaw of widely scattered moving parts all converging on a distant point where everything would click into place to reveal a narrative that moved forwards while its themes went sideways. Until that point was reached, narrative and themes would have to be handled separately; otherwise it was like trying to build the power source of a spaceship with components from its flight deck and vice versa.

Two of our researchers, Jonathan Smith and Chris Walker, took over the task of developing the themes that went sideways. They were promoted to the status of Assistant Producer, fed a glass of cheap champagne each, and locked up in the cell next to mine. While I went off to do a season of *Saturday Night Clive* and another edition of our *Review of the Year* – I had reached the stage where those shows, which required a lot of dedicated graft, felt like a holiday – Smith and Walker cracked the thematic structure, producing masterly documents which explained how fame affected society and society affected fame as the century progressed. Each of their eight main summaries could have been successfully submitted as a PhD thesis except for the complete absence of incomprehensible jargon. Having absorbed these dauntingly profound dossiers, I wisely resolved to adopt as my own every factual discovery they contained, along with most of the conjecture. I had the odd quarrel. Smith and Walker were young – they barely added up to my age put together – and they obviously thought I was a bit of a Cold Warrior still fighting the old battles. They thought, for example, that it was perfectly clear what a bad hat Stalin had been and I would be wasting precious time if I banged on with my favourite theme of how too many intelligent people in the West had allowed themselves to be fooled. But I remembered when it hadn't been obvious. That, for me, was one of the points about fame. It was only a rough guide to reality, but it was a guide we all needed, so it had better lead us in the right direction. In the case of Stalin it had led in the wrong direction, with dire results. Remembering when what was now obvious had still been obscure would be my contribution. So I went back to my cell for another six months and changed everything Smith and Walker had said into my own words. When they squealed too hard I changed some of my words back to something a bit nearer theirs, then changed them back closer to mine again when they weren't looking. They started going to the gymnasium at lunchtime to work off their *angst* on the treadmill.

Finally we got some rough drafts we could agree on and the first programmes went into the cutting room. While the researchers went on gathering material for the later episodes, the early episodes began to form on the editing machines. Editors and their assistants struggled to match pictures to audiotape guide-tracks of the draft scripts read out by myself in hoarse tones. When I walked down the corridor past four of the editing rooms I could hear myself saying four different things. To say that I didn't know whether I was coming or going scarcely registers the feeling. I didn't know whether I was a barber-shop quartet in rehearsal or a bridge tournament dissolving in acrimony.

At the time of writing, the series has entered on its crucial, final stage, when the rough cut heads towards the fine cut in a constant process of swapping pictures to suit words and rejigging words to suit pictures. The more of that you do, the less like a book the script sounds. The commentary of any documentary programme is, or should be, less like an essay than like a song lyric, except that it combines with pictures instead of music. As with a song, the combination becomes a mystery from the moment it happens, no longer analysable and only to be appreciated. If the words are to be read, they had better be typed up at an earlier stage. In this book I have put back quite a few phrases that I had already taken out in the cutting rooms when I realized that the footage made the point. But I haven't tried to go back to the very beginning and write the book as I might have written it if a book had been the only thing I had in mind. Most of the sentences in this text are quite short and very few of them contain a subordinate clause. When writing for a reader you can complicate a sentence by inserting a parenthesis – whether between brackets, commas or, like this one, dashes – and the reader will have no trouble following the argument. When writing for a listener you can't do that without running the risk that he will forget the first bit of the sentence before you get to the last bit. If you want to qualify something, you have to do it next instead of during. The loss is in subtlety. The gain is in speed. The trick is to make the speed subtle. Practice helps, but ('but' is a very useful word in this kind of writing) the main requirement is to be sure of what you are saying. In that regard, as in so many others, I am grateful to everyone on the project. They all had ideas and there was nobody whose brain I didn't pick. The brains were there all day, ripe for the picking. When I got to the office early in the morning there were usually some people still there who had worked all night, and no matter how late I left I had a dozen goodbyes to say, as all those rapidly aging youngsters slogged on, their faces haggard in the spectral light of the monitors and the

VDUs. As with most of the programmes I have ever fronted, I suppose I got into this one, and stayed with it, out of an overweening impulse to say what I know – but it would have been worth doing just for what I was told. Besides, it does a writer good to see what real work looks like. The names of those who did it don't take that long to write down, and even then the list looks twice as long as it ought, because the attrition rate was high: there were some who made it all the way from start to finish, but there were also those who suddenly froze at the VDU some time during the night, and were discovered by the cleaners in the morning. We were never overstaffed, so it was lucky that the staff was over-eager.

In addition to the redoubtable Smith and Walker (concept ramification analysis a speciality), the Assistant Producers were Nigel Leigh, Helen Bettinson, Karen Fulton, Paul Wooding, Manorma Ram, Sue Gagan and Elizabeth Ekberg, of whom the last two became pregnant, but on their own time. Jane Mercer was team leader for Film Research, a business which entails not just the tricky job of finding footage, but the sometimes frustrating job of obtaining permission to use it. The amount of clerical labour involved can soon take the romance out of the task for anyone who lacks patience. On the midnight-oil-burning Mercer task force were Valerie Evans, Carol Davies Foster, Belinda Harris, Anthony Dalton and (there from Day One to the end) Robin Keam. Colin Jones was the first Film Editor on the case, abetted by Paul Willey, Chris Woolley, Richard Brunskill and Christine Garner. Sian Salt found headlines. Joanne King was first assistant to the small, surreptitiously acquisitive Stills unit headed by Maria Chambers, who can find a photograph of anybody anywhere: they don't have to be famous for fifteen minutes, fifteen seconds is plenty.

Requiring as it did the coordination of a monumental amount of information, the series would have been impossible without state-of-the-art word processing technology. Some of the software involved was so far beyond my capacity to understand it that I gave up asking questions and just assumed we could do anything. The Production Assistant was Deborah Black, also doubling as back-up space cadet for the unchallenged princess of the VDUs, Charlotte Wyatt, who tracked the eight episodes through an average of fifteen drafts each without losing control once, except for the day when one of the machines started to underline every word in the building. Preparing the manuscript of this book was merely one of her lighter tasks. I should also mention, while on the subject of how a project this size is made logistically feasible, that our office, which has all our other programmes to deal with as well, would have been reduced by the demands of *Fame* to a smouldering tangle of used plastic and frayed flex if it had not been for the D-Day-harbour-master-standard skills of our Production Managers Bhupinder Kohli and Lynn Hodgkinson. Finally my secretary Wendy Gay, who had more than enough to worry about already, also selflessly doubled as an extra Production Secretary for *Fame* even after she realized that her personal heroine Jayne Mansfield might not make it above the status of the yellow card awarded for a momentary mention – the next category down from a fleeting mention.

One last word before our story starts. Being the book and not the series, it can't begin with Carl Davis's music, Bernard Heyes's title sequence and Ken Ledsham's designs. For those, you'll just have to use your imagination. But it's the right moment to thank the man who has done so much to help me use mine – my dedicatee, Richard Drewett. Once, in one of the many office discussions out of which this series grew, I was trying to pinpoint my belief that fame helps us to make a useful drama out of reality, but only on the understanding that a civilization depends on virtue being pursued for its own sake by the anonymous. The example I chose was the policeman who telephoned me and, instead of saying, 'There's been a car crash but your daughters are both all right', started the sentence by saying, 'Your daughters are both all right.' He thereby saved me from a heart attack and established himself in my mind as the most valuable man I had ever known, though I never knew his name. There was another good example close to hand. Richard Drewett has been Executive Producer on every television programme I have made since 1982, and Beatrice Ballard won't mind my saying that his unmatched critical intelligence has likewise been applied to every word and frame of *Fame in the Twentieth Century*. He bothers about publicity only when the time comes to push a programme, and even then he would rather that the hoopla happened to me than to him. His satisfaction is in the task itself. Achievement without fame can be a good life. Fame without achievement is no life at all. Somewhere between those two principles there is a line of argument. I hope that what you are about to read is it.

BBC White City, 1992

TIME-LAPSE PRELUDE

There was always fame. As long as there have been human beings, there has always been fame. It's a human weakness. No other kind of living creature knows anything about fame, not even the peacock, who certainly craves attention but lacks the brain to know why. In every human group of any size, someone becomes famous, and it's a fair bet this has always been true. When prehistory turned to history, famous people became, almost by definition, the first kind of people posterity got to hear about. Indeed it wasn't until recent times that the writing of history began to concern itself with anyone except famous people and the things they did. Far into the nineteenth century, the famous were remembered and everybody else was forgotten. That was what fame was. It was a classification rather than a force in itself.

But in the twentieth century, fame turned into something different. Suddenly there was more of it. Just when scientific progress was supposed to be ridding the world of myths and ghosts, famous people became larger than life. A special word was brought in for the extra light that the famous were thought to give off: charisma. A lot was heard about the Anonymous Masses. To the extent that they were consulted on the subject, they seemed to agree that anonymity was a drab and undesirable condition. Fame was found increasingly fascinating. And it seemed to happen by public demand. The general spread of education didn't make people more resistant to fame. If anything, it made them *less* resistant.

When the century started, famous people were still required, as of old, to do something first and then get famous for it later. As the century progressed, people who became famous for what they did got more famous just for being famous. Elizabeth Taylor has been famous long enough to exemplify the transition from one state of fame to the other. When she started off, she was famous for being a screen star. In her first big role, in *National Velvet*, when she was still really a child, her heart-shaped face caught the breath of all who saw the movie – and the whole family saw it, usually twice. Her violet eyes looked as if they had been specifically invented to test the possibilities of colour film. When she grew up and appeared as the young bride of the title in *Father of the Bride*, she had the ideal figure to go with the face – perfectly judged, not too much, but the camera couldn't get enough. Even then, some said she was more beautiful than talented. But even if she was just beautiful she could be described as doing something. Today she is famous for being Elizabeth Taylor. She gets married, usually to someone unsuitable. She gets married again, probably to someone more unsuitable. She champions a cause. She brings out a new fragrance. She is very busy – far too busy to make movies. The thing she got famous for is far in the past. Only the fame remains, but it is more attention-getting than ever. It has a life of its own.

To lose the capacity for doing what made you famous in the first place need no longer spell the end of fame. Fame can conquer time. It can conquer death. Elvis Presley is a case in point. The conviction that he is still alive is not confined to California, where a large number of citizens have always been ready to believe that the usual laws of time and space have been suspended or rewritten expressly for their benefit. Shirley MacLaine believes that flying saucers cross space just to land in her backyard. We don't find her belief remarkable. She lives in Malibu and believes everything. But perfectly ordinary people all over the world believe that Elvis still walks among us. There are women leading blameless lives in the western suburbs of Sydney who claim that Elvis makes love to them every Monday afternoon in a motel. He has been seen pushing a trolley in a supermarket outside Basildon, or Brussels, or Bangkok, or Berlin. Elvis Presley's seemingly everlasting fame is part of our reality, for better or for worse.

But how did that come about? It never happened in ancient Rome. Julius Caesar got his face on the coins, but absolutely no Roman rock singer ever made it. Yet, in what is currently the world's most powerful nation, Elvis Presley's face is on the stamps. Why do we need these people? What function do they perform? Sometimes the answer is obvious. We know what function Arnold Schwarzenegger performs. He looks like that so the rest of us won't have to. Most of us don't want to look like a rubber life raft which has been randomly tied up with string before being suddenly inflated and dipped in liquid bronze. We are just glad that he does. He does all that strong-man stuff on our behalf. He is a walking – awkwardly walking – displacement activity. He is also wheeled out to help the

President of the United States win elections. But if he were to run for President himself, Arnie's case would become less simple. He wouldn't be the first actor to be President of the United States. He wouldn't even be the first Austrian to dream about being the world's most powerful man. But questions would arise about the gap between his fame and his qualifications. Or has fame *become* a qualification, proof that you can make it in America, the place where twentieth-century fame started – and where, perhaps, not just chronologically but as a phenomenon, it is now coming to an end?

There are no famous Tibetans except the Dalai Lama, and when the Chinese took over his country he had to leave Tibet, which effectively left it with no famous Tibetans at all. There are few famous Nepalese, they are all called Sherpa something, and Sherpa Tensing is the only one who remained famous after the latest foreign climbing expedition went home. The only Japanese the whole world knows the name of without being told is Yoko Ono. As the century nears its end and Japanese economic power asserts itself, Midori Ito is famous among skating fans, Isao Aoki is famous among golfers, and there are several Japanese Formula One drivers famous among followers of motor sport. But the only truly world-famous Japanese got that way because she married John Lennon. And John Lennon got that way because the Beatles got famous in America.

Twentieth-century fame finally depends on the world's media, a word that didn't exist until long after the thing it stands for got started. It started early. From earliest times, fame and its means of transmission – its media – were intimately involved with one another. But the early means of transmitting fame were of limited range. When people lived in caves, every cave had someone famous in it. But that was as far as his, or her, fame went. There was no way of transmitting it except to write on the cave wall. By the time the cave dwellers found out how to do that, they were already on their way out of the cave, living in bigger and bigger groups that needed kings and queens whose importance had to be drummed into their own people and any other people they might conquer. It could be done by unsophisticated means, such as shouting the monarch's name in unison over and over so that it echoed in the surrounding hills. Or it could be done by sophisticated means: by song, by story, by some form of elementary graven image.

These elementary graven images grew less elementary as time went by. Showcases for them grew more elaborate. The famous person could order a showcase in advance of his own death and so transmit his fame through time. Pit, tumulus, mastaba: there was a steady line of progress in such devices which reached a peak – if the word is not too appropriate – in the pyramid. But as a means of transmitting the Pharaoh's fame the pyramid had one conspicuous drawback. People had to come and see it. They could see it from some distance because it was tall and – for the brief time between the occupant's interment and the arrival of the first thieves – clad in high-quality brick veneer. But it could not be sent to them. Out of sight, out of mind. Yet the pyramid also had a conspicuous virtue: relative permanence. Thus we still remember the name of Cheops, although only the Egyptologists among us know precisely what Cheops did that, say, Rameses II didn't. To the rest of us, Cheops is the man who built the big pointed building. We might guess, correctly, that he got to do that only because he ruled the known world, which at that time extended about a month's chariot ride each side of the Nile. We have only the vaguest idea of what he looked like because portraits at the time were so stylized that one Pharaoh looked pretty much like another: big hat, little beard, things to hold, one foot in front of the other.

A certain amount of time having gone by, Alexander the Great achieved fame for conquering as much of the world as he could reach. His fame was transmitted by several means. His body was embalmed and kept on show in Alexandria, a practice repeated recently with the corpses of Lenin in Moscow and Mao Tse-tung in Peking, and with the same limitations, largely to do with air conditioning. Alexander did better with his contemporary portraits but not much, perhaps because he was always on the move. This vagueness left later artists free to interpret Alexander's features according to their own idea of what the world-conquering hero looked like. The physical image of Alexander the Great has thus altered from age to age. The sixteenth-century Paolo Veronese's Alexander looks rather like the sort of cultivated Venetian nobleman who might have known Paolo Veronese. This tendency of Alexander's image to match the passing moment has culminated, in recent times, with our belief that Alexander the Great looked and behaved like Richard Burton: big head, barrel chest, short legs, weeping because he has no more worlds to conquer, Wales has lost to England at Cardiff Arms Park, and the beer has run out.

After Alexander the pace picked up, although it remained a requirement for world fame that it was hard to get without conquering the world first. Julius Caesar was even better at that than Alexander. Caesar also had the advantage that he built roads, got home more often and was therefore easier to sculpt. As already noted, he got his face on the coins. There was also a bust of him in every prominent niche throughout the Roman world, rather in the way that, until the day before yesterday, there were busts of Lenin almost within sight of each other across the eleven time zones of the Soviet Union. Coins, busts, bas-reliefs and cameos of Julius Caesar all looked at least roughly like the man himself. He also added a promising new device to the range of means by which fame could be transmitted. He wrote his memoirs: the *Commentariorum*.

Unfortunately they were mainly about battles. He has been criticized for not writing even more about the battles instead of digressing to boast about how he could also build bridges. He should have digressed more often. The commentaries would have served him better for containing some of the self-justification that modern politicians go in for. Caesar had a lot to justify: he owned gladiators, for example, until he was forced to sell them. But he said little about himself, so Suetonius and Plutarch could say about him what they pleased. The result was a blurred image. Caesar's fame was transmitted successfully to the future, but his character was left open to interpretation. Shakespeare's Caesar couldn't make his mind up about whether to stay home on the Ides of March as the soothsayer advised. Serious moviegoers in the fifties of our century who saw the Hollywood *Julius Caesar* got the impression that Caesar was a bit of a buffer who looked like Louis Calhern. Less serious moviegoers in the sixties who saw the Hollywood *Cleopatra* got the impression that Caesar was a decisive, tersely eloquent demigod who looked like Rex Harrison. The only consistent impression of Julius Caesar prevailing through the centuries has been the one about how he got famous in the first place – by acquiring a monopoly of power. Along with the power to rule came the means to have one's name propagated, first as an instrument of administration, then – if the man went mad – as an end in itself.

Jesus Christ was the first person to achieve world fame without conquering the world by violence. His message was about another world entirely. The message had a powerful appeal to the down-trodden, which was almost everyone, but it was wide open to misinterpretation. You had to be there to know exactly what he said, and even then you had to be near the

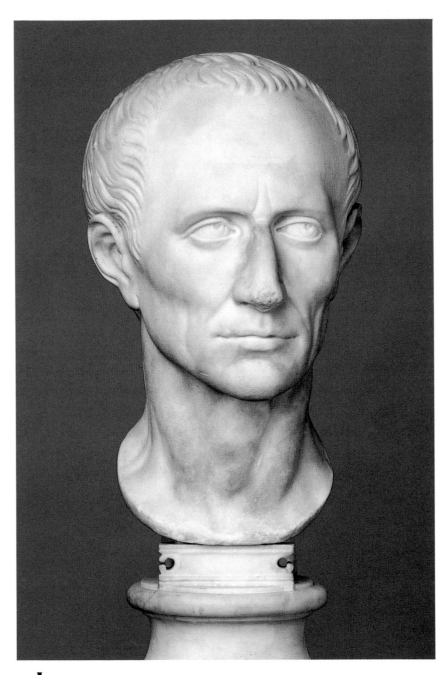

Julius Caesar pioneered many features of modern fame. He wrote memoirs (the *Commentariorum*), spoke in sound-bites ('I came, I saw, I conquered') and formed a David Bowie-style relationship with an exotic famous female (Cleopatra). Some statues suggest a possible cocaine habit.

front of the crowd. Reports written at the time were transmitted far and wide in the form of gospels. They were contradictory, thin on facts, and left the way clear for arguments that depopulated large parts of the allegedly civilized world for centuries. If any contemporary artist rendered the Redeemer's personal appearance, the sketch disintegrated from being passed from hand to hand, so the artists of the future could paint him as they liked, which usually meant the way the local crowds liked. The real Jesus must have been Semitic in appearance but in the anti-Semitic European countries he was usually painted to look Nordic. In our time the same tradition was continued by Hollywood, which, although it was controlled largely by men whose background lay in the Jewish minority, for sound commercial reasons aimed its product at a Gentile audience, the majority. Though the real Jesus probably looked more like Dustin Hoffman, the movie moguls usually favoured such blue-eyed boys as Jeffrey Hunter for the role, shaving his armpits to avoid causing offence. Max von Sydow was a Jesus from the Arctic Circle.

The Dark Ages were a dark age for fame too. Attila the Hun was another world conqueror in the old sense, but all he did was tear things down. He never put anything up, not even a statue to himself. Few eye witnesses survived to say what he looked like. Outside his group of low-life associates, he had no ambitions to be remembered for anything except the usual Hunnish activities – pillage, rapine and pyromania. He burned records rather than kept them, so the picture of his personality was never filled out even to the extent that later ages might speculate about it. Consequently he is just a name, without really being famous at all. Genghis Khan is almost in the same case. He was an Eastern Attila with the same attitude problem. Once again the globetrotting psychopath's chief monument was a long trail of smoking ruins. But since it was well known that Genghis came out of Mongolia, it was possible for future generations to assume with some confidence that his facial structure must have been Mongolian, and so in our time actors of Mongolian appearance – in *The Conqueror* John Wayne wore a Fu Manchu moustache authentically waxed with yak fat – have been convincingly employed to play the part.

Conquering the world with a paintbrush and a chisel instead of the sword and the cross, Michelangelo was the man who spelt the Italian Renaissance to the civilized world, which had grown to be almost as big as the old classical world had been before the barbarians got loose. Michelangelo was keenly interested in his own glory. He thought big: king-sized sculptures, frescoes with a Cinerama spread, a whole ceiling laid out like a curved split screen. He regarded himself as a cut above all those other hacks. Unfortunately he left us no reliable self-portrait beyond a flayed skin in the *Last Judgement*. Though a distinguished poet, he also neglected to write his memoirs, leaving the job principally to Vasari, who was a better writer than painter, though not by much. The consequence once again was lasting fame but little image control, allowing later generations complete latitude to concoct their own version of the greatest graphic artist of all time. The result was almost always a travesty, no matter how noble the initial aims of those who set out to celebrate him. In the film *The Agony and the Ecstasy* Charlton Heston looked magnificent but he had too few lines, while the poetess Vittoria Colonna, played by Diane Cilento, had one line too many: 'Michelangelo, you stink.'

Queen Elizabeth I of England had the same interest in prominent men as Cleopatra but always kept it on a platonic basis, thus preserving her realm. Her emphasis on the judicious husbandry of national resources extended to the control of her own publicity. Prominent playwrights of the period were not encouraged to include any character too closely resembling her in their five-act blank-verse outpourings. The portrait as a means of transmitting fame had always been hampered by how long it took to paint one. With Queen Elizabeth it took even longer because so many finely detailed jewels had to be included. She could write – if she had never been Queen she would still count among the accomplished minor poets of the period – but what she wrote was not for publication. Though word-of-mouth had it that she could be quite merry at court when the Earl of Essex was in town, the impression of the Great Queen that went down to the ages was of a woman hampered by a severe nature. In our time she has invariably been played by actresses with an edge to the voice: Flora Robson, Bette Davis, Glenda Jackson, Margaret Thatcher. They were not given much to go on by their unyielding original. The great ruler thought fame unruly, and kept it on a short leash.

But it was bursting to get loose as more books and periodicals were published. In the next couple of centuries, rulers of various degrees of absoluteness acquired the habit of glorifying themselves by building whole cities – Peter the Great's Petersburg was merely the most conspicuous example – but what really spread their fame was movable type, moving by the million pieces every hour of the day. It could make you famous whether your blood was blue or not. By the early, romantic, unruly nineteenth century, the young poet John Keats wasn't just dreaming of being a great poet, he was dreaming of fame itself. The young poet Byron got what Keats dreamed of. He published a long poem, *Childe Harold's Pilgrimage*, that all the young ladies loved. He woke up to find that he had become famous overnight. From then on, all the young ladies loved him, and not just in Britain but on a European scale. He was written up week by week. The periodicals were making a difference.

Napoleon conquered Europe with the sword instead of the pen. But he realized that fame was a weapon too. He was written about constantly. His portraits took almost as long to turn out as Queen Elizabeth's, because the dedication to simple dress that he started off with gave way to a taste for the sumptuosity that impressed the populace. The huge painting of his coronation as Emperor took so long to complete that he had started rewriting European history all over again before it was finished. But engravings could be quickly turned out for the periodicals and they fixed the essentials of his appearance for all time. Future generations would find it hard to portray him without the proper hairstyle. Nor can any modern impersonator – Herbert Lom, Rod Steiger, Marlon Brando – readily forgo the hand placed in the jacket. Like Julius Caesar's falling sickness or Elizabeth I's reputed baldness in later life, Napoleon's snuggling hand is one of his kit of parts. Images were growing more complex as time went on – still simple, but more like life. Napoleon would have approved. He wanted to be famous, and he wanted his fame to last after death. He was still giving interviews in his final exile.

Only forty years after Napoleon died, Abraham Lincoln was President of the United States. Lincoln didn't especially want to be famous, but by now there was no choice. America's political importance was growing and no politically powerful figure could any longer get out of being famous. If Lincoln was impatient about posing for his portrait, and too busy to meet all but the quickest sketch artists, there was a new device that could capture his image in a matter of minutes. With the advent of photography, fame started to accelerate. Here was a way for a face to be everywhere in almost no time. And it didn't have to hang on the wall, it could just appear in the periodical that came out every week – or,

Queen Elizabeth I of England was an early instance of image management. While she welcomed uncritical masques and pageants in praise of Gloriana, all Elizabethan playwrights including Shakespeare were severely discouraged from portraying the monarch, in however sympathetic a light, on pain of losing their licences and possibly their ears.

It is a sobering thought that while Napoleon couldn't really ride a horse this well, Ronald Reagan could. Even bigger political lies were told in the nineteenth century than in the twentieth, but in the nineteenth it took longer to tell them. In the time it took David to paint a picture like this, Napoleon could rearrange the map of Europe. But there was one technique of modern fame that Napoleon undoubtedly did pioneer: even in exile he granted 'a rare interview' as often as possible.

another new idea, in the newspaper that came out every day. When Lincoln spoke at Gettysburg, hardly anybody was there to hear it. Perhaps it was a good thing. He had a high, not very satisfactory voice, its timbre nothing like as sonorous as his syntax. With no means of transmitting the sound, the speech drifted away on the wind. But when the words appeared in the paper, it was almost like being there, and probably better. It had happened only yesterday. When Lincoln was assassinated, publications all over the country had the news by telegraph, and all over the world not long after. The press was speeding things up. It needed the news.

It needed more news than there was. The popular press really started in Britain. It was the invention of Lord Northcliffe, who realized that mass education had created a mass demand for daily stories. They didn't have to be strictly true, but they did have to be sensational. Soon he had the whole country organized into a single market. The continental countries got the same idea. Soon they all had the beginnings of a national press that could speak to the people about anything, including nationalism. In America, a countrywide press was harder to organize because the country was much bigger. But if it could be organized, the rewards would be bigger too.

Abraham Lincoln's high voice and an unfortunate habit of saying what was actually on his mind would have ruled him out as a President of the United States in the twentieth century.

CHAPTER ONE

THE CLOSE-UP STAKES ITS CLAIM
1900–1927

The outstanding American newspaper tycoon was William Randolph Hearst. He solved the problem of how to satisfy the insatiable public desire for reading about famous people. He did it by making more people famous, building up his friends as saints and branding his enemies as monsters. Later on, by a satisfactory irony, Orson Welles handed Hearst the same treatment by portraying him as *Citizen Kane*. Welles simplified Hearst's character and travestied his long love affair with the actress Marion Davies, who was, in turn, much more talented than Welles portrayed her. But for most of us, Kane and his mistress are all we know of Hearst and Marion Davies. Fame simplifies. It was a process that Hearst himself codified and cashed in on.

At the end of the nineteenth century and the beginning of the twentieth, movable type, moving ever faster, got the new kind of fame off the ground. Pictures went into the papers too. But moving pictures were just a gleam in the laboratory. They flickered and fizzed in the garages and gazebos of gifted amateur scientists all over the world. The country most open to the exploitation of an inventor's discoveries, however, was America, homeland of Thomas Alva Edison.

Edison had his name on two of the principal inventions which would ensure that fame would actually shape twentieth-century history instead of just reflecting it. He invented moving pictures, and he invented recorded sound. At the time not even he thought of joining the two discoveries together. They were fascinating enough separately, especially the moving pictures. Edison enjoyed standing in front of his own camera and did it as often as possible. He was a pioneer of the home movie. But being filmed didn't make him famous. He was already famous for being a fertile inventor of new devices. He didn't necessarily invent what could be done with them, and was capable of violent jealousy if anyone looked like infringing one of his patents. If other people borrowed his moving picture idea to make featurettes for the new Nickelodeons he charmingly sent strong-arm men to smash their

Other countries had inventors too, but America had Thomas Alva Edison, living proof that in America anything could happen. As an inventor Edison was famous in the nineteenth-century style, although if he had realized his film camera was a potent new instrument for generating glory he would have been famous in the twentieth-century style as well, with his personality to the forefront. His other crucial invention for modern fame was recorded sound.

equipment. It never occurred to him that his most extraordinary invention would ever make news by itself.

And at the start it didn't. The first movies were home movies, like Edison's own. Queen Victoria was already the most famous female monarch in the world since her compatriot Elizabeth I. Still photographs of her were displayed in silver frames on top of mahogany pianos in every corner of the world's biggest Empire. In her final hours she made a movie, but it added nothing to her fame. It wasn't seen outside Balmoral. The same applied to the Russian novelist Count Leo Tolstoy. His books were translated while he was still alive. He was as famous as Dickens. The reading public all over the world and many people who had never read anything thicker than a popular newspaper knew that Tolstoy wrote very thick books. The only film footage he had time to appear in didn't make him any more famous. It wasn't news.

Sir Arthur Conan Doyle was a famous British writer who appeared on film. But the film didn't appear anywhere significant. It didn't make him any more famous. The creator of Sherlock Holmes believed in popularity and would have liked to have more of it, but film wasn't a way of getting it. The same went for Rudyard Kipling. He was the most famous of all British writers, read throughout the British Empire. He would have been a natural for film, especially if it could have spoken. If film could have sung, Caruso's fame would have been different. It could scarcely have been bigger. He made some of the first gramophone records, and millions of people who never saw him sing in the opera house did hear him sing at home. Wives who didn't like the noise their husbands made in the bath said, 'Who do you think you are, Caruso?' But a few scraps of film had nothing to do with that. All he did on celluloid was fool around for his friends. It wasn't news.

Getting the motion picture cameras to where the news was happening, getting the film back again to where it could be developed, and then getting the developed film to where it could be shown all needed quick transport, and the means of quick transport were still being invented. When the Wright Brothers made their first flight in 1903 there was no motion picture camera there to catch it. The camera didn't arrive until they flew again. America was too big. Even the fastest of the new automobiles could cross only a little bit of it in a day. For just a moment a small country like France had the advantage. The French had a newsreel system up and running when their most intrepid team of aviators, Louis Blériot and his formidable moustache, prepared to fly the English Channel. Amid maximum *tohu-bohu*, the French for brouhaha, Blériot set off to battle the air resistance created by his formidable moustache. He made it and became world-famous. But he *stayed* world-famous only in France. He didn't make fame a career. He was content to be a French national hero.

Madame Curie was a French national heroine. She discovered radium, an extremely glamorous substance which gave off mysterious rays that journalists enjoyed writing about. She wasn't glamorous herself, but she didn't care. She won the Nobel Prize and every other prize and was proud of her calling. But she wasn't interested in fame. She had nothing to tell the reporters except a lot of stuff about radioactivity. Thirty years had to go by before the Americans finally managed to immortalize her by replacing the unglamorous reality with a glamorous fiction that the audience could appreciate. Greer Garson starred as *Madame Curie* with Walter Pidgeon as her husband Pierre. It was one of a string of movies known to the trade as Garson–Pidgeons, and neither Garson nor the studio had any intention of making the great scientist look realistically haggard. Instead, they made her 'human'. The real Madame Curie already was human, and the Greer Garson version transparently wasn't, but that was what fame did – it simplified what was real so that people could take it in. In America, where the people ruled, the century was only a few years old when an ambitious politician realized the possibilities.

Teddy Roosevelt started his build-up to the Presidency by gleefully cooperating with any printed organ which would run his photograph. He smelt votes and his whiskers bristled. He was so vibrant that the pictures almost moved. When the pictures *did* move, Teddy was quick to get into them. He was a complicated, brainy man who realized that a simple, manly image would win him fame and fame would win him elections. He got the emphasis off his politics and on to his personality, away from the intellect. A visionary who foresaw America's global dominance, he took steps to embody it personally, creating the first Presidential photo-opportunity for a motion picture camera, which proved to be an opportunity for the cameraman to be almost flattened by a falling tree. Tireless, shameless, a machine for converting energy into publicity and vice versa, Teddy the White Hunter strode forward to world fame over the dead bodies of thousands of animals. In real life he had a tender regard for nature and set up some of the first conservation areas. But he preferred to be famous as a wild man of the woods, slapping aside all opposition like his favourite animal, the grizzly bear.

Teddy Roosevelt set a trend for twentieth-century American Presidents to play the role as much as they filled the office. It was with his example in mind that Presidents learned to be performers – Franklin Delano Roosevelt, Eisenhower, Nixon, Kennedy. Later a performer learned to be President – Ronald Reagan. Looking back, it seems logical that if a President of the United States turned himself into a star he would open a window of opportunity through which a star would one day emerge as President of the United States. But stardom had a long way to go before that happened.

In the early 1900s, the people in the movies were just little figures on the screen, smaller than the people who were sitting in the dark watching. But then something happened that turned twentieth-century fame into something else: the close-up. It made cinematograph performers into stars. It could make anyone into a star. Twentieth-century fame isn't just about Hollywood. Some of the most famous people of the century never made a movie. But they have all been *in* the movies, because one of the things that made them famous was the film camera's capacity to make the face so big. Larger than life, different from life, it took on more meaning than it had in reality. A new and strange relationship was established between those looked at and those doing the looking. It had something to do with eroticism, although the close-up brought the onlooker into a greater intimacy with the looked-on than could be achieved by any lover, who would always have his imagination kept in check by the actual texture of a living thing. With the close-up film face there was no limit to the imagination's involvement. Radiant in the distance yet close enough to taste, the people in close-up were symbolic, but what they symbolized was the people watching them. It was a way for the human race to worship itself in ideal form. It still is. It happens in public, but it's as private as self-love. When Madonna strokes herself on camera she is merely putting her finger on this fact. And if it's one-way, it doesn't *feel* that way. You know these people so well that you can't believe they don't know you.

They don't, of course. They never did. Nobody could become a star without being cut

At the beginning of the century Teddy Roosevelt had already embraced all the techniques of twentieth-century fame including the photo opportunity. He condemned all subsequent Presidents to the necessity of dressing up and showing aggression, although none of them shot as many animals as he did, partly because he left so few animals alive. In reality he was a highly literate man interested in wildlife conservation, but the image, with his active encouragement, took him over.

Sarah Bernhardt contemplates her sad fate in being born too early. Famous as an actress inside and outside France, she was famous only as a *French* actress. Film would have made the world her country, but by the time it was ready for her she was no longer in her first youth. Her funeral in Paris ranked for pomp with that of Victor Hugo, whom she had known quite well.

off from the mass of people who were going to buy the tickets. Twentieth-century fame has tended to unite bigger and bigger audiences while making those who possess it more isolated. The process began early, with the Hollywood star system. When the close-up came in, old-style acting ability went out. It was useful, but it wasn't essential. Even the greatest actors on the stage wouldn't necessarily make it in the movies. The nineteenth-century-famous French actress Sarah Bernhardt was on her last legs when she starred as the dying Queen Elizabeth, so it was perhaps unfair to describe her late bid for screen fame as a flop. Unfair, but accurate. Isadora Duncan was another nineteenth-century hangover. Famous for dancing in an untutored, not to say unhinged, manner, she managed to get herself filmed doing it, but proved by doing so that it would be easier to turn someone more photogenic into a dancer than a dancer into someone more photogenic.

What was essential was looks. Perfectly ordinary people who looked good turned up in Hollywood from all over America and soon from all over the world. A few of them were cut out of the herd and became stars. In those very first years of the close-up, between 1908 and 1910, a huge audience could recognize the Biograph Girl but they didn't know her name. The Biograph studio issued a statement denying that Florence Lawrence had been killed in a streetcar accident. Actually no one had ever suggested that she had. It was a publicity stunt staged by the studio. It worked. Florence Lawrence became a famous, if not very likely, name. It was the beginning of the star system. Studios had to have stars. When the stars realized how necessary they were, their salaries went up, from five dollars a week to five hundred times that much in the first four years. The studios paid out, not just because they couldn't do without the stars, but because big money kept the stars on a short leash. They couldn't do without it. They felt the same way about their fame.

Francis X. Bushman. William S. Hart. Theda Bara, whose name was an anagram for Arab Death. Most of them are now forgotten. At the time they were part of the scenery. Some of them acted like it, but they were all heroes. They looked like heroes. They presented an insoluble problem to real heroes who wanted to become stars. Buffalo Bill, after a glittering late nineteenth-century career of slaughtering buffalo, had movies made about himself. But he didn't look as much like a cowboy as the screen cowboys did. Houdini, the great escapologist, had a fitful screen career based on his skills as a man who could get out of

Houdini the escapologist was one of the first famous people of the century to encounter a potentially fatal problem: the over-enthusiastic fan. One of them who had read about his highly trained abdominal muscles hit him in the stomach when he wasn't ready, thereby hastening his demise.

anything given a certain amount of time. But he couldn't get out of the problem posed by the fact that his real ability to escape from impossible situations was irrelevant on the screen, where the stunt could be faked using an actor who looked better than he did. By the time his career ended he was only pretending to go over Niagara, a silent admission that someone with more screen presence could have been doing the same thing. Stars had to fit their fame. Looking the part was what they did. They were up there looking handsome, or looking lovely. It was easy for them to look handsome and lovely because that was what they were. But they also had to look intelligent, innocent, passionate, sensitive, heroic. Above all, heroic: in control of life on behalf of the audience, who weren't.

Twentieth-century fame – this new centripetal/centrifugal force which seemed to suck everything into showbusiness before squirting it out again – was still confined to America. The rest of the world might have heard it throbbing, threatening to burst out. But the rest of the world didn't yet rate America that high. Still thinking of America as a provincial place where a washed-up act went to make money, Europe continued producing the old-style heroes – real ones who actually did things, even if they didn't do them very well.

Intrepid if inept, none was more heroic than Britain's redoubtable Antarctic explorer Robert Falcon Scott. Though hopeless when it came to the petty practical details which merely meant the difference between life and death for his colleagues, Scott was aware of the value of publicity and took film cameras with him as far south as he could. But he died out of reach of the lens, leaving only a diary. The diary later became a best-seller and helped to establish Scott as a hero in the old style, waging a private, lonely interior battle with destiny. His blunders were forgotten. He was enshrined as an example of the best type of British officer, with a stiff, indeed frozen, upper lip. He was an example to his class and later in the century became the embodiment of his nation, when the whole disastrous expedition was staged all over again at Ealing Studios. The moment when John Mills, peering through snow-caked binoculars, descried the fateful Norwegian flag at the other side of the studio, is a proud memory for all those who were brought up on a diet of British films after World War II. Mills, as Scott, said it all in one word: 'Amundsen.' The other guy had got there first.

Roald Amundsen was an even less likely candidate for twentieth-century fame than Scott,

Scott of the Antarctic (below), arriving second at the South Pole, won fame beyond the dreams, or the aims, of the man who arrived first. Though largely a result of his gift for mismanagement, the tragic deaths of Scott and his men provided the British press with a better story than mere success.

The Norwegian explorer Roald Amundsen (above) reached the South Pole first. Travelling light, unqueasily prepared to eat any dog that had grown too tired to drag him, he made sensible plans and got his men home safely. To the world's press he was dull copy and his subsequent fame was confined mainly to Norway.

since he had got on with the job, reached the Pole first, and returned without fanfare to become famous in Norway. But even Scott is less famous outside his country than the people inside his country tend to think. The British like him because he was decent about coming second. He was a national hero, and there was already something outdated about national heroes. Though the European countries were slow to realize it, twentieth-century fame was international, even if most of it was in America, which had already developed the infuriating habit of treating itself as if it were the whole world. Sophisticated Americans – the novelist Henry James was a prominent representative of the trend – were appalled by such confident provincialism and took refuge in Europe, thus helping to lull sophisticated Europeans into the belief that America was all noise. But the noise was made by a giant stirring.

The World Heavyweight Boxing Championship became an American monopoly when Jack Johnson revealed a frightening ability to obliterate all opposition from other countries. America's white men didn't like it when Johnson went out with white women. They locked him up for it. They dreamed that a white version would show up. The journalists had a name for him: the Great White Hope. He would, of course, be American. America seemed as good as the rest of the world put together, perhaps because it *was* the rest of the world put together.

The point was rubbed in when World War I started. It was strictly a European event. America wasn't interested. As the slaughter commenced, the news was dominated by nineteenth-century-style moustaches. Behind them were the men in charge, but you could hardly see them. Kaiser Wilhelm II was the chief German moustache. Reputedly he was crazy, but it was hard to tell. The next most famous German moustache was Hindenburg. He was meant to be a pitiless Hun like Attila, but if his cruel lips were twisted with ruthlessness there was no way of telling. The top French moustache was Marshal Foch. He was billed as a military genius and might have looked like one without all the facial hair. Great Britain's leading moustache was King George V. With a beard to complement his moustache, he was known to all by name yet utterly invisible.

Britain's Prime Ministerial moustache was Lloyd George. He was a brilliant orator but since there was no sound film or any radio at the time you had to be there to hear him; and he wasn't there in the front line, he was safely at home seducing women. Britain's top military moustache was Lord Kitchener. He inspected the troops while the troops did their best to inspect him, but he was hard to see. The hero of a poster, he was like a poster himself. He was stuck up, and when he was lost at sea he was taken down.

As the total of dead mounted into the millions, gradually it became apparent that the great moustaches wouldn't do as heroes. The fighting man was the hero. He had to be a hero every day for as long as he lasted. But he didn't look like one. The average soldier was covered in mud. The average soldier was dead. Individuals were hard to find. They showed up above the battlefield, in the form of ace pilots. Germany made a hero out of Baron Von Richthofen, the Red Knight of the Air, so called because he flew into action in a little red Fokker triplane. In the clean arena high above the muddy massacre, single aerial combat looked like chivalry. Actually the war in the air was mainly a matter of shooting the other guy in the back if you could, but at least it looked as if a man could show honour to a gallant opponent, survive by skill, and die on his own terms. For purposes of raising morale, the German high command poured on the publicity. Richthofen became a hero to all Germany. Though portrayed as a dastard by the Allied press, he became a bit of a hero to our side as well, symbolizing human individuality in a war that had wiped it out. The Australian soldiers who shot him down gave him a hero's funeral. After the war the Germans dug him up and buried him all over again.

The Red Baron was above the battle, in a neat little war of his own. The same sort of thing was also permitted at the *edge* of the battle, in obscure places such as the Middle East, stamping ground of Lawrence of Arabia. He was T. E. Lawrence, a gigantic ego well camouflaged as a neurotically shy, short man. He had a knack for backing nervously into the limelight. The limelight was mainly provided by the American journalist Lowell Thomas. He sent back reports about this exotic Englishman who dressed up as an Arab prince and went tearing around the desert like Sir Galahad in a sheet. Thomas played up the story for all, and more than, it was worth, hitching his wagon to Lawrence's romantic star. America was suitably intrigued, but the exotic Englishman's heroic stature was of importance mainly to the English. Lawrence was a national hero. Aided by a gift for telling tales as elaborately decorated as his presentation jewelled dagger, he had made the war look like old-fashioned derring-do. Peace was less exciting. Either genuinely revolted by his publicity or aiming for

Lawrence of Arabia dressed like this in order to mingle unobtrusively among the natives. His exploits in the desert were carried to the world by a press hungry for tales of adventure. When the press needed help he supplied details out of an active imagination. He lied like Hemingway, walked away from fame like Garbo, and crashed to death like James Dean. His autobiography *Seven Pillars of Wisdom* was the first famous book of the century which everybody bought and nobody finished.

legendary status, or both, he tried to hide from his fame under various assumed names, eventually killing himself on a powerful motorcycle. At the time his passing was noted mainly by his friends: the British ruling class for whom he had been a golden boy. His true fame only happened forty years later, when the movie came out. Though they had cast the part of one of the world's shortest heroes with one of the world's tallest actors, Peter O'Toole was at least British, or at any rate Irish. The film had a British director, David Lean. But it was an American movie, arriving late at the event and taking it over.

Boycotted by America, World War I went on exterminating its own extras in the modern manner without producing any stars who didn't look old hat. The Russian Revolution did better. It produced Lenin. Or rather, Lenin produced it. And he produced it in every sense. Lenin staged the Revolution as a theatrical event as well as a political one. If he didn't personally arrange to give himself top billing, it was only because he didn't have to. Dutiful *apparatchik*s did it for him, making him the centre of attention for a propaganda system which right from the start was the most efficient thing in the Soviet Union apart from the secret police. Lenin was cast as the symbol of centralized and unquestioned power, the embodiment of a new civilization which would replace the old Western version. It never quite did, but for most of the century it ran as an alternative.

His own people cast him as a demigod. After his early death they rained tears into his open coffin, all unaware that he was never going to go away. The corpse was never buried. Lenin's face was used for a death-mask which became the mould for a million reproductions. First gradually, then grotesquely, after death Lenin was raised to divine status. On permanent display inside his aggressively hideous mausoleum under the Kremlin wall, Lenin's corpse, pumped full of artificial preservatives, became Moscow's longest-running hit show.

State-run fame had its limitations, but in the early days they didn't obtrude. Otherwise intelligent people in the West didn't mind that Lenin backed up his orders with a gun because they approved of his management skills. In the West as in the East, it was widely assumed that scientific management could fix anything and lead the world to progress. Henry Ford put his name on the century like no one else. He put America on wheels and the whole world followed. He turned the automobile from a privileged carriage into a mass-market consumer utensil. He was hailed as a genius with a vision of the new, infinitely

З.И. Ленин

In his role as the embodiment of the Russian Revolution, Lenin was helped by considerable histrionic ability and a prescient understanding of how the means of communication could be coerced into transmitting a simplified image. He made a point of comporting himself as a man too busy to look at the camera. Since the natural thing to do with a camera is to look at it, to behave as if it is not there is the mark of a ham actor, but the public didn't know that. After his death his brain was found to be sclerotic but was cut up for study anyway, in the hope that the secret of genius might be discovered in its molecular structure. Unlike Stalin's, Lenin's fame as a champion of social justice survived the collapse of the Soviet Union, despite his frank statement that the Party would have to rule by terror, and his energy in constructing the apparatus which would ensure that it did.

mobile democratic society. The Ford Motor Company *was* the new America. Ford's success at creating an industrial empire was so enormous that delusions of genius came drifting with the smoke from his factories to his house. His fame went to his head. He rated himself as an original thinker on world affairs. His critics were nearer the mark when they called him an anti-Semite and a hayseed. In his saner moments he seemed to agree that the backwoods were where he belonged. He had home movies made in which he featured as a simple soul communing with the elements. In old age, when he seized the microphone and spoke, he just didn't match up to his own historical significance. Though Henry Ford had done more than Lenin to shape the twentieth century, his voice came quavering out of the nineteenth, when what a man did was what counted and his personality didn't have to match his renown.

No less an industrial centre than Ford's Detroit, Hollywood was more up-to-date. The star system's production line turned out personalities too good for this world. Stardom was a parallel world ruled by the people in it, with no one below the rank of prince and princess. The king and queen were Douglas Fairbanks and Mary Pickford. Pickford was America's sweetheart: she had innocence, along with a salary of 350000 dollars a picture. Fairbanks was the athletic hero. He had athleticism, and teeth. Even off-screen the couple were on-screen, living in a house on a hill that was like a castle where all the world's famous people came to pay court. On-screen, the couple were a fairytale. They chose their costumes from the vast walk-in wardrobe of the romantic past. They were modern heroes, but the heroes they played were a hangover from another era.

The same applied to Rudolph Valentino. No man in history had aroused so much female desire. But he looked as if he came from history, or anyway from somewhere exotic. He was a gaucho who danced the tango. He was a bullfighter who got gored. But mainly he was *The Sheik*. He was Lawrence of Arabia with a degree in Latin American dancing. He was something else. Valentino was equipped with a smouldering glance that could reach all the way to the cheap seats and scorch the spit curl on a flapper's forehead to a frazzled pretzel. Valentino had a violinist's hands, which the camera dwelt on as his female fans dreamed of being held like a Stradivarius at various strategic angles. For the studio publicity department Rudi was gold dust. They set up sex appeal tests to measure his cataclysmic effect on the

Rudolph Valentino as *The Sheik*, with a well brought up young abductee bravely facing, along with countless millions of female cinemagoers all over the world, the delicious prospect of being ravished by the century's most famous Great Lover in the days before date rape became an issue.

43

Charlie Chaplin was the first great example of twentieth-century fame and the first to realize that it was a force to be managed, not to say manipulated. Some critics *did* say he was a manipulator and down-rated him as a comedian, but his fellow comedians knew better. 'He's a goddamn ballet dancer,' said W. C. Fields, 'and if I get my hands on him I'll kill him.'

female metabolism. Off-screen, Valentino was obliged to keep up his performance as a great lover with magic powers of sexual attraction and infinite supplies of *savoir faire*. In real life he had been a male taxi dancer and freelance lounge-lizard, but real life had been left far behind. He was in over his head. When he tried to take control of his own movies he had one financial disaster after another. He found out that he was a prisoner of his fame. The public wanted *The Sheik*.

He came back as *Son of the Sheik*. They had changed the girl but it was the same tent. He knew his way around it blindfold, and barring accidents he would have gone on to make *Grandson of the Sheik* and *Sheik Trek V: The Voyage Home*, perpetually transporting upper-class young women over a sand dune for immoral purposes, his palpitating victim the object of toxic envy from untold millions of watching women as she echoed the curve of the Great Lover's dagger while he bent her to his will on cushions hot from the sand beneath.

Valentino was merely the most sensational example of a performer whose real-life personality became confused with an outlandish persona. The man and the role were two different things, and it was becoming evident that if the man couldn't control the role, the role would control the man. Fatty Arbuckle lost control. Famous for his screen portrayals of a little boy who got into trouble, in real life he got into trouble like a little boy, but he did it with big girls. Arrested after a girl died at a party in circumstances that were never made clear, Arbuckle was destroyed by the press before he could be tried. His career as an artist was over because he hadn't managed it like a businessman. Fame needed a clear head.

Charlie Chaplin grasped this fact and became the first truly great figure of twentieth-century fame. His role as *The Tramp* wasn't drawn from the romantic past, or from some exotic land where they danced the tango in Arab head-dress. The Tramp was from the twentieth century. Thanks to the nearly universal reach of silent film, he was the most recognizable figure on Earth. And the man who played the role made himself famous too. Chaplin enthusiastically cooperated with the publicity that built him up as a genius who had the whole picture under his personal supervision. With the fame of the real man added to the fame of the role he created, Chaplin filled the sky as the most famous person in the world. There had never been fame on that scale before. When Chaplin toured his native England it wasn't like going home; it was like going to a foreign country – the fame country, which started just outside his front gate in Hollywood and covered the whole planet, full of people who wanted to shake his hand but didn't care if it bled.

The price of adulation was isolation. Chaplin found himself cut off from the mass of mankind that adored him. Only other famous people could behave naturally in his presence. Lord and Lady Mountbatten, making an early start on a long career of being noble friends to the famous, asked to be included in a private movie. Chaplin and Douglas Fairbanks were like little boys together because they *were* little boys together, living again the last time when they might have met each other by accident. Cut off from ordinary people, the film stars were trapped with each other, paying for the upkeep of high walls to shut the public out. When Fairbanks and Pickford toured Europe, they found to their horror that their loving public was ready to crush the life out of them. There was no way back from this kind of fame. Anyone who got it was stuck with it. Unprecedented fame brought unprecedented problems which not even the smartest stars could yet guess at. They had to find out the hard way.

All except one woman, who seemed to have the whole thing figured out in advance. Her name was Greta Gustafsson and she started off by being famous in Sweden. She was a substantial girl with a disarmingly natural set of teeth. But she had something – a ticket to America. After a change of name and a rewarding encounter with a cosmetic dentist, Greta Garbo held America enthralled. Americans knew Sweden was in Europe somewhere and Europe was where women were aloof, blasé and so sophisticated they made love with the light on. This wasn't Mary Pickford looking winsome in a dirndl. This was sexual desire. *Flesh and the Devil* was the very first time the American screen had shown a kiss happening horizontally, the way they did it in Europe. The movies were still silent but Garbo's silence was eloquent. It didn't just say 'Your place or mine?'; it said 'Your place *and* mine.'

It was widely assumed that Garbo and her favourite co-star John Gilbert were not acting. This was especially easy to believe in Gilbert's case. He fell in love with her off-screen. So did romantics of both sexes in dark cinemas everywhere. Garbo moved love to the ethereal level for millions of ordinary people all over the world who didn't have much time for love on any level. She made them see what they were missing. She did it for them. She never complained when the studio stills photographers made her pose for hours while they angled

Garbo refused to cooperate with publicity stunts but always willingly sat for the studio photographers when they angled lights to purify even further the planes of her face, an edifice which, as Bernard Berenson said of Raphael, reflects back to us the classicism of our yearnings. When the MGM executives woke up to the fact that she was just as keen to maximize their expensive asset as they were, she was given an unprecedented say in the management of her career. Whether her eventual retirement into silence was a ploy to guard her mystery, however, is doubtful. She might simply have had the sense – in a famous person the rarest gift of all – to quit while she was ahead.

lights to reduce her face to the minimum of information. She understood exactly what they were after: ideal sex. Garbo firmly squashed all attempts by the studio to invent a private life for her. The studio soon got the point. Mystery made her a bigger star. If the studio couldn't publicize her private life, it could publicize her reluctance to reveal it. It was the enigma effect. Whether she calculated this effect, or whether she just found all the hoo-hah too silly to get mixed up in, remains a mystery to this day – like almost everything else about her.

But few famous people were as instinctively wary about their fame as Garbo. They had to learn. Everybody did. It has taken us a whole century of fame to find out that its radiance burns. Fame has to be handled with care. It needs special suits and lead shields so that people can step into all that light and still breathe. As Chaplin had already guessed, the real story of twentieth-century fame would be how to live with it. But that didn't become clear until someone died of it.

It was Valentino. If he had been operated on in time, he might have been saved, but they couldn't find a surgeon to match his prestige. It was the last farce of his life. His death was a theatrical triumph. People queued to get in. The funeral rites started in New York, where the queue to see his body became a riot. Valentino's body crossed the country by train. The funeral in Hollywood was one of the film world's events of the century, razzmatazz in mourning. But for millions of women all over the world his loss was the occasion of deep and lasting grief, which pundits preferred to call mass hysteria, rather than face the difficult question of how otherwise normal people could feel love for a dreamed object, passion for an illusion, and treat the life and death of a man who wore funny hats as if it was a matter of life and death. It was the death of innocence. Fame was a force, and the proof was in the coffin.

CHAPTER TWO

ALL AHEAD WARP FACTOR ONE

1918–1932

As the years between the wars began, America wasn't yet the deciding factor in twentieth-century fame. Older countries still had their pride, and could prove it. They were bang up-to-date. Suzanne Lenglen was five times Wimbledon Singles Champion. If she had entered for the Olympic high jump she would have won that too. She wasn't American, she was French. Anna Pavlova toured the world with her *Dance of the Dying Swan*. The swan died a thousand times to overwhelming applause. She wasn't American, she was Russian. Dame Nellie Melba, no longer in her first youth but still energetic, made the world's first radio broadcast. The toast named after her is still consumed to this day. She wasn't American, she was Australian. And those were just some of the women among scores of women and men from various countries who all came to world prominence. Language was ceasing to be a barrier. News could be translated, and anyway in a new activity like international competitive tennis language scarcely mattered. Now that the possibility of leisure had been extended beyond the leisured class, the number of things someone could be famous for had increased.

America's intervention had finished World War I. Economically the old Empires were already dead. But they wouldn't lie down. Right through the 1920s the British turned out a supply of famous people to keep their Empire suitably enthralled. Using various means of transport, first Sir Malcolm Campbell and then Sir Henry Seagrave, or vice versa, repeatedly broke the world record for maximum publicity over the measured mile. Amy Johnson flew solo all the way to Australia. When she got there she spoke a language the Australians understood, although it didn't sound like their language or any other language spoken by an ordinary human being. She sounded as if her mother had been to school with Queen Mary. It was the language of Empire.

The British Empire was one big happy family because most of its children were seen and not heard. But they were allowed to play together even if they were different colours. The

Australia's own nomination for the title of Favourite Son, Donald Bradman scored hundreds of runs at such a rate, and with such style, that he turned cricket into a dream for spectators and a nightmare for the other team. Eventually the England bowlers slowed him down by bowling at his head – a concept known as Fair Play. Bradman never cashed in on his fame, living out his life quietly as a successful stockbroker. In America such reticence would have been impossible – but then, so would cricket.

American troops on Pacific islands during World War II knew that a *banzai* charge was on its way when they heard Japanese soldiers crying: 'Death to Babe Ruth!' The Japanese played baseball but Ruth was famous even in countries where they didn't. Since he often had trouble making the weight, he would have been the right man after whom to name America's most popular candy bar, but in fact it was named after the manufacturer's daughter.

game they played was called cricket, and only people who belonged to the British Empire could understand it. England was the heart of the Empire, so it was only fitting that the dogged English batsman Jack Hobbs should put the natives in their place by scoring hundreds of runs against Australia. But the English were very sporting about it when the natives fought back and Australia's Don Bradman scored hundreds of runs against England. It wasn't until the following decade that they tried to put him out of action by throwing the ball at his head, a tactic strangely known as 'Bodyline' instead of 'Headline'.

Nobody outside the British Empire had any idea why these men were running backwards and forwards or talking a lot of incomprehensible jargon about hitting each other in the bails with a googly to the inside leg. The famous names of cricket were famous as far as the Empire went and no further. Since the Empire went quite far, it was practically world fame. But in America a sportsman achieved world fame in a sport played scarcely anywhere else except in his own country. Babe Ruth was the greatest name in baseball. He won the World Series for the Yankees. Cricket-loving cynics in Britain might have said there was nobody else in the world series *except* Yankees but at least the British got to hear about him, whereas no American ever got to hear about Jack Hobbs or Donald Bradman. The reason was that Babe Ruth wasn't just good at baseball, he was good at being a celebrity.

The celebrity was yet another pioneering American contribution to twentieth-century fame. Celebrities weren't just famous for what they did. They were famous for the lives they led while they did it. As American sports became more and more professional, the professional sportsman found that he wasn't famous just when he was hitting or running, he was famous when he was at home eating, or out drinking, or running off the rails. The celebrity sportsman was famous for being human. Babe Ruth was human in a big way. In 1921 his signing-on fee for the Yankees was 125 000 dollars and he had already spent half of it on hotdogs. An America hungry for Babe Ruth statistics was told how many hotdogs he ate and how fast, along with how many home runs he hit and how often. His fame didn't just have quality, it had quantity. When the Babe had trouble making the weight, it reassured American men who had trouble waking for work. Babe Ruth helped to make baseball grow big. Baseball got written into the plots of movies, so Babe Ruth was heard about even in countries that never took the game up. One of the countries that did take the game up was

Japan, so that later on, during World War II, American troops on the Pacific islands heard Japanese soldiers shout during the night that Babe Ruth would die in the morning.

America made its national sporting heroes into international celebrities. And boxing was an international sport, so when an American won the World Heavyweight Championship there was nowhere on earth he wasn't a household name, whether the house was made of brick, wood, palm leaves, dried mud or ice. The name was Jack Dempsey. Boxing went legal in 1919 and turned into big business. Dempsey was a famously mean fighter who got more famous the meaner he behaved. The public was fascinated with the idea of a man who would hit below the belt even when his opponent was already lying down. Dempsey's character was a big draw. He wasn't just a famous boxer, he was a famous brute. So he was famous twice. When Dempsey had been on top for seven years he lost his title to Gene Tunney and failed to regain it after the notorious long count incident about which every boxing buff will give you the boring details unless you get in fast with some cricket statistics. But the important thing was that Dempsey accepted defeat gracefully. He stopped being Mr Nasty and started being Mr Nice. He became famous for that too. So he was famous three times.

Dempsey *stayed* famous. Even out of the ring, he was still courted by other famous people. Charlie Chaplin wanted to know him. When they pretended to fight, Douglas Fairbanks was the referee. Dempsey didn't get very far with his film career but that became part of the story too. Later on Dempsey lost all his money in the Stock Market Crash and *that* was part of the story. He staged a comeback as a restaurant owner and other famous people came to eat. Dempsey survived as a performer even when he ceased to be a champion. He fought his way free of what he did, and became somebody who simply *was*.

Sporting celebrities, any kind of celebrities, were like film stars, with less of the mystery but aspiring to the same durability. They didn't just do something once. They did it again. They were still news even when they weren't doing it. They were there all the time. It was getting harder for anyone to perform a single heroic feat and then quietly retire. Heroes were now expected not only to risk their lives but to hand their lives over to the hungry media. The day of the lonely hero was almost done. At that very moment, the greatest lonely hero in history performed his death-defying feat.

Jack Dempsey won fame as the World Heavyweight Champion who could be depended on to fight with thrilling ruthlessness. After the famous Long Count incident he earned a belated reputation for sportsmanship. He had a nose-job to become a film actor, lost his money in the Wall Street Crash, made a comeback as a restaurant owner, and generally proved that a boxer's fame didn't have to end with his last fight.

The first to fly the Atlantic alone, Charles Lindbergh was the ideal hero until the press realized
that he didn't want to cooperate – some said out of shyness, others out of arrogance. His fame
brought on the kidnapping and murder of his baby. Bitterness and an unfortunate admiration for
Nazi Germany led him to use his fame against President F. D. Roosevelt in an attempt to keep
America out of World War II. After the war started he was not allowed to fly in combat but
reputedly shot down a Japanese fighter while on a fact-finding mission. He lived out his career in
aviation pioneering routes for Pan Am, eventually achieving again the obscurity
he was so sorry he ever left.

54

At first glance, Charles Lindbergh was a gift from heaven for the omnivorous new means of mass communication. He let them do all the communicating. He never said a word. But he was as good-looking as any film star and his wings didn't come from the prop department. He was real. He was patriotic. He was perfect. The whole of America flew with him across the Atlantic. His progress was tracked on the London, Amsterdam and Tokyo stock exchange tickertapes. The country built by Europe's rejects was sending its sensationally brave son on a voyage of conquest in reverse. When he arrived in Europe it was like Columbus coming back, all on his own. The French went crazy. But the Lone Eagle was soon looking trapped.

The press and the newsreels believed that they had helped to build Lindbergh up and there was something to it. The Lone Eagle had never been entirely alone. The idea of flying solo across the Atlantic wasn't a lonely dream, it was a competition with 25 000 dollars in prize money. It could have been won by someone else. It could have been won by René Fonck, a French war hero whose attempt to fly the Atlantic was foiled only because he took too many croissants with him. The plane was too heavy to take off. If he had travelled light, the name of Fonck would have resounded through the twentieth century. You could call it the Fonck Factor. The single heroic deed could always be done by another person. So the media couldn't help believing that Lindbergh owed them something when they called him a hero. They wanted cooperation in return.

The story started going sour when Lindbergh didn't give it to them. He came home to a hero's welcome which was staged twice. First he came home to Washington. Battleships sank under the weight of photographers. Then he came home to New York. More than 4 million people turned out to see him. The tickertape formed drifts knee-deep to cushion the fall of fainting secretaries. It was hype, and it made him unhappy. He had to fight hard to keep smiling. Before his great flight to immortality his taciturnity had been a plus. Now it was a minus. The media which had sung hosannas to his silence now wanted him to say something, and the same silence looked like ingratitude. He was the same man but the rules had changed. The media wanted the show to go on. Its hero wanted it to be over. The perfect hero was a dud celebrity. The Lone Eagle was laying an egg.

Lindbergh didn't *enjoy* fame, so there was no story there. He had done his deed and

America's most famous gangster, Al Capone played the role of a Borgia prince to such effect that Hollywood leading men have ever since clamoured for the part as the next best thing to appearing in tights and a velvet cape. In Chicago it is hard to enter a bar without encountering people who once knew him intimately. How did he ever manage to kill anyone if they are all still alive?

there was no bigger deed left to do: the only comparably astonishing one-trip flight left to make was to the moon. So there was no story there either. The only story left was his private life. Lindbergh wanted to keep it private. The press tried to intrude and he tried to keep them out. So *that* was the story. He couldn't hide, so he tried to run. But when Lindbergh and his new wife arrived in Japan, the cameras were waiting. His search for obscurity was transmitted to the waiting world. The Lone Eagle was already finding to his cost that twentieth-century fame was a show you couldn't get out of once you had been cast in a starring role. He just didn't want to be in the limelight.

But there were plenty of people who did. Prohibition made America's gangsters into headline news. The bad guys became big celebrities. Scarface Al Capone was the baddest guy, so he became the biggest celebrity. He loved the part and dressed up for it. The media couldn't get enough of him. All they had to do was turn on the lights and he did the rest. He paid for his own wardrobe. Extras to play dead bodies he provided free. He made his own transportation arrangements. His car was built to stop bullets from other gangsters. The cops never shot at it. They just gave lectures about it, pointing out its exciting features: armour plate, bullet-proof windshield, standard-issue police siren – this last doubtless provided, although the police press liaison officer didn't say so, by one of the cops on Capone's payroll.

Compared to the cops he had corrupted with payoffs, Capone looked honest. Apart from the people who were actually getting beaten up or rubbed out, the whole world seemed to like the idea that at least one man was up there above the daily grind. Capone liked the idea, too. His fame justified him. He was beyond good and evil. He was in showbusiness. He wasn't really a killer at all, he was more a kind of star. As if to prove the point, the film studios rewrote his life a dozen different ways; but it was always the same part, the big part, the American equivalent of *King Lear*. Film stars wanting to play it formed a queue seventy years long: Paul Muni, Edward G. Robinson, Rod Steiger, Al Pacino, Robert De Niro. They changed the story and they changed the setting and sometimes they even changed Capone's name, but it was still him. Capone is a classic. He's lasted longer than Lindbergh and it's because fame suited him. He *needed* fame. It was a step up.

It was a step up for honest people too. The great black jazz musicians were down there in the lowlife of Prohibition America, and if they wanted the status they had coming to them they had to go with the story. The only problem was how far. When Louis Armstrong's long career ended he was the most famous jazz musician in the world. For millions of people who didn't know much about jazz, he was the voice and the face they knew. People who *did* know about jazz said that he had thrown away his art and there was nothing left except showmanship. But they seldom asked why that was. The answer was that when the man famous for singing 'Wonderful World' was starting off, the world wasn't so wonderful. In Prohibition America the black inventors of the twentieth century's most exciting music had the same prestige as minstrels. Armstrong's brilliant trumpet solos were works of art from a sweatshop. The works of art were preserved on classic records. All over the world people with a true, unprejudiced ear for musical creativity heard the 78rpm recordings of Armstrong's Hot Five numbers and delightedly recognized a great musician. The dramatically improved means of its transmission had made Armstrong's world fame safe from the start. But in the land where he lived, white men controlled the record business and stole most of the money. To stay solvent, the artist had to become an entertainer. Louis Armstrong the revolutionary modern musician turned into Satchmo the showman. Out on the road night after night, Armstrong clowned it up. But if he was wearing a false face, at least he had made it himself. When Hollywood put him in the movies, they put him in costume. Armstrong loathed the jungle-bunny outfits and the Uncle Tom dialogue, but it was the price of fame. And fame was the road to freedom. Black entertainers couldn't raise their status without being celebrities. That meant they had to have a story. Armstrong's story was the one about the man full of spontaneous joy. The price of celebrity was to be stuck in the role. Armstrong had to be hail-fellow-well-met no matter what.

For a black American artist in the 1920s, it was hard to become a celebrity without being typecast, not just because he was black but because in America any artist had the same problem. No one who became famous through achievement could stay famous without giving the media a story to feed on. The only hope was to control the story. Duke Ellington understood that it wasn't enough to be a serious musician. He had to *behave* like a serious musician. He was an entertainer too, and never lost sight of the necessity to please the crowd, but he thought that his prestige as a composer was good business and the best

In his early years
Louis Armstrong
recorded trumpet solos
that rate amongst the
most beautiful modern
music of any type. By the end
of his long life he was America's
roving jazz ambassador to the world.
In between, his music became less
interesting as his fame increased. Showmanship
was more marketable than artistry and Armstrong was
in no position to buck the market, but later
black musicians who made jazz a symbol of
rebellion couldn't have done it if Armstrong
hadn't helped to make it so popular in
the first place.

Albert Einstein published his most revolutionary scientific papers when he was still an obscure patent official in Switzerland. Other formative twentieth-century mathematicians and physicists – Planck, Dirac, Bohr, Fermi, Heisenberg – remained obscure. Einstein achieved world fame, largely because of the popular though erroneous notion that his theories of relativity had some relevance to ordinary life. Einstein's world fame was an embarrassing burden to him but it came in useful when his letter to President Roosevelt, warning that it would be possible to build an atomic bomb, was immediately read and acted upon – a clear case of fame affecting history. People who don't know their twelve times table know that $E = mc^2$.

weapon against prejudice. Even in the movies he managed to keep his dignity. For the white men who were out to exploit black talent, black dignity was an obstacle. Ellington's smile never slipped, but his eyes showed that the cost was high. Though fame had made it possible to take his art to a wider world, fame had also made him a representative of his people: a responsibility that no white musician was asked to bear. In America it was the fate of black success first to be feared by white failure, then to bear the weight of black aspirations, and finally to be accused by black power of playing Uncle Tom in a white man's world. It took a strong man to carry a load like that and keep swinging. Ellington never missed a beat.

Duke Ellington had a long career ahead of him as a cultural hero, but in America that was the hardest kind of hero to be. The mass media weren't interested in the artistic achievement. They wanted to hear about the interesting life. If the person of achievement wasn't prepared to be a celebrity, there was no story. In that respect Europe still had America beaten. In Europe someone who did something didn't have to do it for the media first. Achievement was saluted by an elite and the reputation arrived later.

In Vienna, Sigmund Freud developed a complicated theory about how the unconscious determined behaviour. His name was known to everyone who could read. The press made him world-famous by simplifying what he had to say, until eventually everyone in the world who could only just read came to believe that Freud thought sexual repression was bad for you. This message was especially popular in American speakeasies late at night. But Freud was famous in Europe first.

In Berlin, Albert Einstein developed the General Theory of Relativity. He was admired by the scientific community and lionized by the social elite. The press made him world-famous by spreading the vague notion that Einstein said everything was relative, so anything went. This message was especially popular in America, where pseudo-scientific cults were beginning to challenge evangelical Christianity for the allegiance of the would-be profound. But Einstein was famous in Europe first.

In the great cities of Europe, America still seemed far away. From Paris it was a dot on the horizon. America had the money, but as far as culture went Lindbergh might as well have stayed home. There were famous Americans who agreed with this assessment. They made Paris their stamping ground. None stamped more effectively than the girl who wore bananas for a skirt. Josephine Baker was black, sassy, and sexy off-stage as well as on. The American media would have destroyed her. In Paris they loved her. She could be her real self without having to invent a false one. She tore the place apart.

The fame of the young American writer Ernest Hemingway began in Paris. He went there to write about the condition of modern man and journalists went there to write about him. He was there because a few dollars bought a lot of francs and because America was too small for him. He wanted to be famous, but on his terms. The fame of the young American writer F. Scott Fitzgerald increased in Paris. At home he had written a book about drunken young wastrels – *This Side of Paradise* – and attained celebrity for behaving like one of his characters. In Europe he drank no less but he acquired class. In Europe writers were taken so seriously that they made news, and he liked being in the news.

The Americans were in Paris because they thought their own country was too provincial. The Russians were in Paris because their old civilization had vanished into the pit dug for it by Lenin. The Russian composer Igor Stravinsky had come from old Petersburg to knock Paris dead with *The Firebird*, *Petroushka* and *The Rite of Spring*, which caused an uproar that made his name synonymous with the kind of music your mother thought was incomprehensible noise. After the Bolshevik Revolution, Petersburg turned into Leningrad and Stravinsky made Paris his address. The Irish writer James Joyce was in Paris because his own country banned his books and in Paris the dollars he borrowed from his rich American female patrons bought more whisky and cigars. In Paris he published the kind of novel your mother thought was incomprehensible filth. And Pablo Picasso was in Paris because if he had stayed in Spain his early struggles might have gone on for the rest of his life. In Paris he fulfilled himself creatively and was a big hit at the same time. The American expatriate Gertrude Stein helped make him world-famous for painting the kind of pictures your mother thought were incomprehensible daubs. But in Paris the elite were either clever enough to understand him or scared of looking stupid if they said they didn't.

In Paris to be smart was smart. Paris was an all-star spectacular of brilliant foreigners who were there for the exchange rate, the tolerance, the intelligence and the style. The style was set, however, by a local girl. Coco Chanel invented the little suit – *prêt-à-porter*, ready-to-wear – that made style affordable for women who weren't rich. Her *couture* clothes made

As a black singer and dancer whose act depended on uninhibited sexuality, Josephine Baker would have had a low life expectancy in her native America, but in Paris she was an instant hit, and lived on to become a national institution. The famous novelist Simenon was among her lovers. Less lucky with her husbands, she compensated by adopting children from all over the world – an early Mia Farrow situation which resulted in financial difficulties. She joined the Resistance during World War II, as distinct from other entertainers who joined it after the war was over.

Coco Chanel came up from nowhere to make Paris fashion into an international industry and herself into a new kind of aristocrat. Realizing that journalists preferred to be supplied with excerpts ready made, she flattered worshipful young poets into composing such epigrams for her as: 'Luxury is a necessity that starts where necessity stops.' Living by her own rules, she overdid it during World War II when she had a love affair with a German general, but after a period of exile in Switzerland she was eventually welcomed back by a Paris that couldn't do without her.

the rich feel richer. She made the fashionable feel artistic. She made fashion into a new set of values more valuable than a pedigree, as if to have chic was a birthright better than birth. Chanel herself was raised in an orphanage and at the peak of her fame turned down the hand of the Duke of Westminster, although she had already become intimately acquainted with the rest of him. Reputedly she said, 'There can be many Duchesses of Westminster, but there is only one Chanel.' A lot of the things she reputedly said were written for her by adoring young poets and essayists whom she kept close and threw crumbs to. In realizing that the best way to get usefully quoted by journalists was to feed them a prepared excerpt, Chanel was ahead of her time.

Chanel also perfected the technique of putting exclusivity on the open market. Her fragrance Chanel No. 5 was sold on the idea that only the discerning few knew about it. In fact it was available to anyone who could afford the equivalent of 215 dollars an ounce in today's money. Chanel raised design to the level of art and herself to the level of artist. Though Hollywood had plenty of dress designers, in 1931 Chanel was brought over to contribute the extra something that America was still convinced only Paris could do. Chanel graciously agreed to spend an entire year in Hollywood's barbaric atmosphere, with only a small hill of money for compensation.

In the twenties the news from Paris got to America within the month because the Paris editions of the new glossy magazines like *Vogue* and *Harpers* were owned in America. American money bought European style. The Europeans thought they were getting the best of the bargain, protecting their traditional cultures and getting paid for it. British actors enjoyed the prestige generated by speaking a version of the English language that Americans applauded for its sophistication. 'And how was China?' asked Gertie. 'Very big,' replied Noël.

In 1925 Noël Coward had three plays on in London. But the West End was just an out-of-town try-out for New York. He starred in his own plays on Broadway too. It was where the fame was. European theatrical stars had once toured America to make money when they were washed up. Now they came at the height of their careers. Broadway was bigger than London as a showcase for theatrical stars. Hollywood was bigger than either but it couldn't talk: not until October 1927, when *The Jazz Singer*, a movie with only half a

Gertrude Lawrence rewards Noël Coward for having written some of her most successful stage roles. Gertie inevitably dated but Noël – whether as playwright, composer, lyricist, actor or cabaret artiste – went on and on, living long enough to go out of fashion and come back in again at least twice. He compressed one of the great lessons of twentieth-century fame into an epigram: 'The secret of success is the capacity to survive failure.'

soundtrack, revealed the full talent of Al Jolson. Jolson already had national fame as a Broadway musical star whose stock-in-trade was the kind of energy that couldn't be stopped with gunfire and a blackface act that graphically demonstrated what Louis Armstrong and Duke Ellington were up against. It never occurred to Jolson that he was being racist. But it takes only a few bars of Jolson's 'Mammy' to remind us why Josephine Baker had to go to Paris. It was a wonder she didn't go to Patagonia.

Sound film turned Jolson from a crass vaudeville headliner into a world-famous crass vaudeville headliner. He gave it everything he had, so he had nothing left over for the audience to wonder about. Sound movies threatened the mystery of silent stars. It didn't matter to comedians. Laurel and Hardy were just as funny throwing noisy pies as quiet ones, and there was the bonus that Hardy could say something, even if Laurel still didn't say much.

The Marx Brothers would have remained stars of radio and Broadway if it hadn't been for sound film. Harpo was essentially a silent comedian plus a motor horn. But Groucho talked. He had always been written up as a famous wit. Now the cinema audience could judge for itself how witty he was. It was through the movies that Groucho established his world fame as a master of the wisecrack. Self-exiled in London, the American-born poet T. S. Eliot might otherwise never have come to admire him. As it was, the two men formed a lasting friendship. It was a hint that world fame could be a kind of community in itself.

If he had the right things to say, a famous comedian could deliver on his reputation for being funny. But a famous woman of mystery could be killed off by the wrong dialogue. Garbo was aware of the danger, and planned her own transition to sound very carefully, choosing a part – the title role in *Anna Christie* – where her Swedish accent worked for her instead of against and saying as little as possible even then. She still let her face do most of the speaking. It spoke the real feelings underneath the words, as if the words were just part of the decor. But what she *did* say she said in a foreign accent, and a foreign accent spelt sophistication. The result was a big success, although observers who managed to retain their objectivity – she was one of them – knew that the days were over when she could transcend a trite story. From now on the scripts would have to be as good as she was. When MGM made plans for her they found her a willing, even demanding, conspirator. Translating her drawing power into influence, she participated in the management of her own career.

Garbo's redoubled fame suggested that the sophisticated European stars whose accents were just foreign enough still had a future in American movies, especially if they could sing. Whether Marlene Dietrich could *really* sing is a question that can still provoke fisticuffs, but whatever it was she did it didn't sound like anything home-grown. Dietrich outdid even Garbo in the European-style sensuality stakes. She was *really* exotic. In *Morocco* her American-born leading man was just dressed that way. He was plain, bashful Gary Cooper and he wasn't used to this sort of thing. She blew his mind.

The Hollywood stars of European origin were actually helping America to export its own version of the world – a version which would be unrecognizable in their countries of origin. But at the time it looked as if the imported exotica were filling a need that the Americans couldn't fill themselves. One of the first Hollywood musicals, *Love Me Tonight*, was about Paris, and it seemed only fitting to import the biggest musical star in France, Maurice Chevalier. Directed by Rouben Mamoulian, another import from Europe, the film had a fluency which belied the clumsiness of early sound equipment: the swaggering Chevalier looked and sounded right at home. But as far as the studio was concerned, Chevalier was the unknown risk. The sure bet was his co-star, Jeanette MacDonald, and she was a native-born American.

Jeanette MacDonald was a huge star at the time and she was soon matched with a huge male co-star, Nelson Eddy. So even when the musical was set in some outlandish landscape, two Americans were singing at each other nose to nose. Sophisticated Americans called MacDonald and Eddy the Iron Butterfly and the Singing Capon. But unsophisticated Americans were buying the cinema tickets. As the Depression turned into a disaster, the demand for entertainment went up and the studios were ready to try anything that worked. Sex was high on the list. It turned out that sex didn't have to be European.

Jean Harlow was a sexy American. She looked like a man's idea of a woman with nothing else on her mind. But she could act as if she had a mind of her own. Famous straightaway for her erotic charge, she might have added lasting fame for portraying characters with brains to match their bodies. But she died young, and even if she had lived she wouldn't have been writing her own dialogue. It was always written to suit men.

Nobody did a more thorough job of being the European sophisticate in naive America than Marlene Dietrich, who was famous in a different way for almost every decade of the century, without ever ceasing to be herself – there was a strong intelligence underlying the perpetual transformations. In the thirties she was famous for wearing the clothes of both sexes. Half a century later, after her death, she became famous again for having *been* both sexes: the secret she had never hidden had finally come out.

Mae West was already a veteran of innuendo-laden theatricality when she was launched on her brief heyday in the movies. It ended when Hollywood lowered the boom on sexual suggestiveness, but until then she left the other girls for dead with her racy dialogue, much of which she wrote herself. But she never actually said: 'Come up and see me sometime.' She was still making screen comebacks forty years later, an object of admiration for those who believed that her first screen appearance was already a comeback, and that she had been George Washington's mistress.

Some experts said that Mae West was a man. Others said that she had been George Washington's mistress. But nobody ever said anything as good as what she said. She supplied much of her own dialogue and delivered it with enough eyeball-rolling suggestiveness to disguise the fact that she didn't really look very sexy, she just sounded it. Her style was *innuendo con brio*. Garbo's sensual appeal was based on the assumption that her personality was a castle with no drawbridge: a successful suitor would have to climb the ivy. With Mae West there was a highway to the front door. She had a sharp tongue which could tell Cary Grant to go jump in the lake or else to come up and see her sometime – the latter phrase being one she never pronounced in those exact words, but that's the way the phrase got famous, in a not uncommon instance of the folk memory supplying the rhythm that the original lacked.

People had to be told that Cary Grant came from England. They thought he was just an American who talked in a sophisticated manner. America had absorbed enough European class and gloss. Now it was producing its own. But there was a big difference. American classiness was classless. It was aimed at the masses, with no apologies.

America's Stravinsky was George Gershwin. He had all the talent of a composer in the classical tradition. If he had been European it would have been a scandal for him to get mixed up in the musical theatre. As an American, he took to Broadway without missing a beat. He took it over. He loved it all: the razzmatazz and the fame. He loved the girls and they loved him right back. When Hollywood called, Gershwin answered. All over the world, Gershwin's admirers feared that he would be overwhelmed by too many parties and pretty girls. Gershwin was only afraid that he wouldn't. Hollywood wanted popular songs from him and that's what he wanted to give them. He didn't think his art was being corrupted. He thought it was being developed.

He was right. American popular art had always had energy, but now it had eloquence. It could provide a setting for the American popular hero that made him irresistible, even if, like Fred Astaire, he had few of the attributes of the pre-sound matinee idol. Astaire didn't look all that different from the ordinary guy in the audience. He could do extraordinary things, but he did them in a natural way, with no histrionics. He was exceptional yet nothing set him apart. What he did was superlative without being superior. He had lyricism, but with words you could sing. Fred Astaire and Ginger Rogers were sexy, but only with their feet, like butterflies. Nothing threatening, nothing to shut you out. This wasn't the high life behind closed doors – it was high spirits out in the open. The Astaire dance poem was the sheer expression of uncomplicated joy. Projected all over the planet by Hollywood's worldwide distribution system, it made America look like a democratic paradise where a shy guy with an ordinary face like his could dance like that and get a girl like her.

Astaire acted shy on screen. But he could get away with acting shy off-screen only because the system was protecting him. Shyness fitted his ordinary-guy image, so the studio's enormous publicity apparatus was deliberately geared down to give the showbiz reporters just enough to keep them happy. Charles Lindbergh, who really *was* the shy American hero – or anyway seemed to be, although some who came into contact with him said he was merely arrogant – was wide open. The press just kept on coming, because unless he flew around the world upside down without stopping they had no other story except his strange desire for privacy. Lindbergh was too normal to get the point. He wasn't enough of an actor. He and his wife dutifully posed for photo-opportunities celebrating the arrival of their baby. Lindbergh honestly thought that if he gave the press something today they would stay away tomorrow. But as Lindbergh found out in the cruellest possible manner, the real trouble wasn't with the papers and magazines that printed the family photos, it was with some of the people who read them. Some of them were more than just curious. A few of them were crazy. And one of the crazy ones was a killer. When the Lindbergh baby was kidnapped, the biggest story of the century, the one about the lonely flyer, took off all over again. The media did the same sort of job on him that they had done before. The indiscriminate nature of twentieth-century fame was clearly demonstrated to anyone cool enough to take stock.

But no one was that cool. Everyone climbed aboard the bandwagon. Al Capone, in prison at the time, offered a reward for the kidnapper's apprehension. When the baby's body was found, the Lindbergh legend took on a new, permanent lease of life, through death. Lindbergh had always been in the difficult position of a private man at the centre of a public event. Now the difficult position had become impossible. At the trial, the alleged killer was Bruno Hauptmann. He was the first in a regrettably long line of twentieth-century assassins who achieved celebrity by murdering celebrities. Hauptmann almost certainly didn't do it.

The best proof that fame in America could be much more than ballyhoo, and that popular art could be Art, Fred Astaire confined his efforts to being the great innovative dancer of the screen and every songwriter's favourite singer. Off screen he never did much except blush, stammer and conserve his energy. The consequence was a long career and untarnished fame.

The victim was so famous that the police had to find a killer in a hurry. But there was no doubt about who was really in the dock. It was the star witness. Lindbergh was the victim, but he was put on trial. He knew none of this disaster would have happened if he had not been famous, and now disaster was making him more famous still. Private grief was public property. The Lindberghs had not only lost their baby's life, they had lost theirs.

Famous Americans were already worried that the fans might overwhelm them. Now they had to face the possibility that, among the autograph hounds who pressed forward without seeming to understand they might crush their prey to death, there might be some who *did* understand it, and who wanted it that way, and who studied the magazine photographs of the famous person's lovely new house looking for a way in. Fame American-style suddenly looked helpless, like America itself. In Europe a new breed of hero had more contempt than ever for America's culture of the common man. The uncommon man was on his way. A new aviator was due to drop out of the sky, and this one – Adolf Hitler – wasn't shy in the least.

CHAPTER THREE

THE CHARISMA KIDS
1930-1939

In the 1930s, to be famous in Europe was to be famous enough. The educated classes of Europe still looked down on America as a kind of kindergarten. The 1929 Wall Street stock market crash had led to a worldwide Depression that made capitalism look like a failure. Economic upheaval was an American export, but no solutions were forthcoming from the site of the catastrophe. The real politics were in Europe, where various competing ideologies were heading forward to Socialism, back to Nationalism, sideways to National Socialism. It would take a strong man to stave off chaos. A superman. There were various supermen available. The daddy of them all was Benito Mussolini, *il Duce* – the Leader.

Mussolini had already been strutting his stuff since 1922, when he led the Fascist march on Rome and found a power vacuum into which he expanded like a balloon full of hot air. But Mussolini wasn't all talk. His first claim to fame was that he made the trains run on time, a feat he accomplished by beating up a few carefully chosen helpless victims. He was also a master of the judicious murder – not on a mass scale, just the carefully chosen liberal opponent – and of the technique, much practised in the ancient Rome he was out to restore, of gaining credit as a champion of law and order by purging his own thugs once they had finished the job of frightening everyone else. But he was *almost* all talk. Fascism depended on appealing to the people by turning politics into a show in which they had a permanent role as extras. Mussolini played most of the leading characters himself. The superman was a statesman. He was a horseman. He was a musical genius. He designed his own costumes. He showed a particular flair with hats. He also knew when to take his clothes off in order to display his magnificent torso.

It was common knowledge that women of every class, even the aristocrats, found him irresistible, although his sexual technique was said to consist mainly of throwing them to the floor and passing over them in a shallow dive. The sensual aspect of his super powers didn't show up on the newsreels, but everything else did. The Fascist movement was

Everybody's favourite Fascist dictator, Mussolini won his first fame
for making the trains run on time. Murdering only a carefully chosen few
liberal opponents, he attracted more praise than opprobrium from international
political observers who admired the supposed hardness of his huge head. Even his
colonial adventure in Africa might have been forgiven if he had not made the fatal
mistake of believing the publicity he received for his political genius. But he
persuaded himself that teaming up with Hitler was a sure bet instead of a
gamble. He forgot that he was in showbusiness.

essentially a movie by Cecil B. De Mille. When sound came in, Mussolini took all the speaking parts. The cast of millions had nothing else to do except turn up on time and shout agreement. If they forgot to come in on cue, he agreed with himself, thrusting his massive jaw in the air and shaking it vigorously, like a killer whale short of a toothpick.

Though it wasn't wise to say so, there were plenty of people in Italy who guessed that Mussolini's heart was in showbusiness. But there were a lot more people who forgave his histrionics because they thought history was on his side. Some of them lived in other countries and were famous themselves. The Irish playwright and pundit George Bernard Shaw was a hangover from the nineteenth century who had achieved twentieth-century fame for his piercing insight. He praised Mussolini for his powers of decision. Shaw was well aware that these powers of decision were dictatorial. He was rather fond of that idea, too. The Dictator was an actor and Shaw liked drama. He and *il Duce* were *dramatis personae*.

But intellectuals like Shaw weren't the only non-Italian admirers of Mussolini. There was a German politician who watched everything Mussolini did with a mixture of excitement, envy and a conviction that he could do even better. In 1933 Adolf Hitler conquered Germany with a bigger show than Mussolini had ever dreamed of. Booked in for a long run under the title of the Thousand Year Reich, Hitler's mega-budget spectacular was a monster musical that included the audience in its choreography. Hitler was a self-proclaimed super-man with an irresistible appeal, because he persuaded his followers that *they* were supermen as well. For the price of a ticket, they weren't just entertained, they were transformed. The trick was made plausible because Hitler had so successfully transformed himself. He didn't look like a superman, but that was the point. He was up from nowhere and could have been anybody. What made him unique, in his own eyes and in the minds of all who fell under his sway, was his willpower.

Hitler raved on about a new race of seven-foot-tall, blue-eyed blondes with big muscles and even bigger husbands. His own personal appearance was rendered significant only by the flopping cow-lick, the dust-bug moustache, and the pointed eyeballs common among people for whom anti-Semitism counts as a complex political theory. Yet his admirers, numbered in the millions, never noticed the contradiction. He mesmerized them.

In normal circumstances Hitler would have been just another headcase writing to the

The most powerful single piece of evidence for the theory that personalities affect history, Adolf Hitler aimed to replace Germany with himself. His paramilitary formations swore loyalty to him personally. Later on the armed services were obliged to do the same. The Nazi seizure of power would have been inconceivable without him and when he was dead Nazi Germany survived him by only a few hours. He died in the belief that the German people had been unworthy of his destiny. His fame lives on as the century's supreme example of absolute evil, although there is a case for believing that Stalin and Mao Tse-tung were even more toxic, since at least Hitler never pretended to be creating a just society and frankly announced his intention of exterminating the unfit. Widespread belief that he would do what he said was slow in coming, hampered by the accurate perception that he was histrionic to the roots: he had already worked out lighting designs to suit himself when he was still a semi-student living hand to mouth in Vienna.

newspapers complaining that his wolfhound had been given indigestion by a passing child. But circumstances weren't normal. Sabotaged from both the left and the right, a weak state had left itself wide open to a bold man driven by big dreams, and one of his biggest dreams was fame. Hitler had always been interested in fame. As a semi-student in Vienna it had been the only thing he ever studied seriously. Hanging around the public library with a liverwurst sandwich in his raincoat pocket, he sketched lighting designs that would make him look like a man of destiny.

By the time he got his show on the road, he had taken on some help. Hitler was like a film star with a personal staff. In charge of all Hitler's publicity was Josef Goebbels, who had a highly effective method of making sure that Hitler was always the main topic of all means of communication – anyone who showed insufficient enthusiasm for his client, he simply threatened with sudden death. There are press agents today who would like to have the same clout but they lack the back-up. Goebbels' chief advantage was a docile client. Hitler was always ready to cooperate with the machinery of publicity. Even in his home movies he was willing to do another take if the cameraman muffed the first one.

Another prominent staff member was Rudolph Hess. Still dizzy from his privileged position as the private secretary who had been allowed to transcribe Hitler's prose masterpiece *Mein Kampf* as it poured from its creator's inspired lips, after the Nazis came to power Hess got the vital job of acting as Hitler's feed-man and adoring stooge. At rallies, Hess pioneered the technique later used on American television talk shows whereby a feed-man plays dumb so that the host can act smart. Whipped into a frenzy by Hess, the audience was already orgasmic with enthusiasm before Hitler even opened his mouth.

But for an artist to attract top-class advice he must first have talent, and that was what Hitler had. He was a ham actor but he had timing. It was his idea to enter a rally always from the rear of the auditorium, so that he appeared to emerge from among the people as the expression of their desires, the embodiment of their dreams about a better fate. And above all he knew how to time a speech. In this department he improved on Mussolini, whose speeches started big and stayed big, sharing the formal properties of a salami. Hitler started small. He started by not talking at all, while the audience – already driven berserk by Hess – gradually calmed down. Waiting, Hitler looked like an ordinary man faced with too big a task. The audience grew apprehensive. What if he gave up, went home to Austria, changed back into lederhosen and spent the rest of his life raising wolfhounds? All Germany held its breath as one. Into the silence Hitler launched his first soft words, the grammar dubious, the sentiments execrable, but the voice, even at such a low pitch, already as brain-curdling as Kulminator, the most fatal brew of the Munich Beer Festival.

As the hour-long speech progressed, Hitler pretended to draw energy from the adoring crowd in the arena and the millions of theoretically enthralled listeners clustered around the radios at home. He became an extraordinary man, a man possessed, gripped by his tremendous vision of a superior Aryan race battling against the world Jewish-Bolshevik conspiracy to invade Germany and open a kosher restaurant flying the hammer and sickle on every street corner. To the detached observer he looked like a six-year-old boy throwing a tantrum in tight underpants. But at the time it was hard to remain a detached observer. Even the cleverest people thought that Hitler really must be some kind of superman after all. Once again, Bernard Shaw avowed that he admired a dictator's powers of decision. People who knew Hitler was evil were still impressed by his success. He was supremely powerful and he was supremely famous. He had the power to declare himself famous, so it was easy to combine the two things.

In America they were still separate. Power was in Washington and fame was in Hollywood. The only fully equipped American superman was in the movies: Tarzan of the Apes. Tarzan's ape-call was based on a Tyrolean yodel. If Johnny Weissmuller, like his parents, had been born in Germany, he would have provided Hitler with a stunning example of what the master race looked like with its clothes off. But Weissmuller was raised in America and got the job of Tarzan instead.

He started off as an Olympic swimmer who won so many gold medals he could stay fit just carrying them around. He was a revolutionary technician of his chosen sport, perfecting a whole new style in which the chest served as an aquaplane. He wrote an excellent book about the subject which can be recommended as a useful guide to the concentration of effort required for success in any field of endeavour at all. But there was no future for an amateur competitive swimmer, and there *was* a future for a good-looking young man who could swim.

A piece of Greek sculpture with an outboard motor, Johnny Weissmuller had a face matched for classical beauty only by Marlon Brando and Elvis Presley. The lavishing of all that on the undemanding role of Tarzan was a measure of the extravagant resources available to American popular culture. Weissmuller played Tarzan for a salary and didn't own a piece of the action until he played Jungle Jim, by which time unwise eating and the tax officials had caught up with him. He died broke in Acapulco.

Weissmuller had a face off the front porch of the Parthenon. He was a natural to play the king of the jungle. In one low-budget movie after another he fought to gain the upper hand over Tarzan's deadly enemy – the dialogue. As everyone remembers it, the most famous exchange of dialogue in a Tarzan movie – 'Me Tarzan, you Jane' – wildly overestimates the complexity of what he actually said. He said: 'Tarzan. Jane.' But his double looked good somersaulting through the prop vines and he himself swam beautifully, especially in the underwater scenes, which were filmed with a simple lyricism never matched later with budgets ten times as big. This was where dreams of omnipotence belonged: in dreamland. The king of the jungle was a sportsman turned actor and the jungle he was king of was a hundred yards across at its widest point. Everybody was enchanted and nobody was fooled, not even the ape, who wasn't earning all that much less than Weissmuller.

In Europe, the eyebrows of the highbrows were raised in derision at America's culture of daydreams. But there was one big advantage in confining daydreams to culture. It kept them out of politics. In America, the man in charge didn't have to be a superman. Franklin Delano Roosevelt would have been better cast in the role of superman than any of the European dictators. But he didn't want the part. He left all that stuff to Tarzan. Roosevelt was a different sort of strong man. The human consequences of the Depression were standing in line for work: any work. People with nothing were trapped by little debts. Roosevelt's New Deal was a bold plan for rescue, and it would have been easy for him to agree when he was hailed as a saviour. He preferred to present himself as an ordinary man and play the drama down. But it was still drama. When he said that there was nothing to fear but fear itself, Roosevelt didn't scream or throw his right hand in the air, but he was still a showman. His common-man routine was carefully rehearsed.

The real Roosevelt was an aristocrat. If America had a ruling elite, he belonged to it. His unquestioned and unself-questioning membership of the upper stratum was one of his strengths, because he knew the rich for what they were and suffered from no insecurities when he told them that the time had come for them to think of the common good. Yet if Roosevelt had merely exercised his silver-tongued oratorical skills on a privileged audience he would have stayed remote, like Woodrow Wilson. What made Roosevelt exceptional was his revolutionary trick of talking intimately to everybody all at once. He did it through the radio, in a regular feature known as the Fireside Chat.

Though a recording of it might sound stilted by the folksy standards of a later, more practised age, Roosevelt's Fireside Chat was fundamentally different from a dictator's ranting broadcast. FDR wasn't out to establish his own superiority. He wanted the listeners to appreciate *their* importance, not his. At any rate he made it sound as if he did. There was an element of flattery. But there was a bigger element of fraternity. One common man was speaking to all the others, as if it was only a fluke that had put him where he was.

The press knew that FDR was a showman. They forgave him because it was a great show. The press knew that FDR had been crippled by polio and couldn't stand up without leg braces, but they never talked about it. Even when he appeared on behalf of polio charities the effects of the disease on him were never mentioned. It takes less than a minute to see all the film footage showing the extent of FDR's affliction that has ever reached the screen.

FDR didn't want his condition to become an issue and the media agreed. It was also known to his inner circle that he was unfaithful to his wife Eleanor, the most famous First Lady of the century. She was a woman who would probably have been famous without him, a condition which she might well sometimes have pined for. Roosevelt was far from being a perfect man. Forty years later he would never have been elected. In the long run FDR's very success in making himself so famous helped to ensure that no candidate for the Presidency of the United States could hope to escape the full glare of media attention. At the time, though, a president could still afford to be fallible. It was part of his charm. In the era of the superhumans, he sounded human.

Radio was a medium that favoured the common touch. In the dictatorships the radio *had* to run the leader's speeches and the population *had* to listen. In America, even FDR had to compete for an audience on the open market. The worst that the radio could inflict on the audience was too many fervent requests to buy dog food, or, some said, too many songs by Bing Crosby.

Bing's singing sounded so much easier than other people's singing that it was called crooning. Actually there was an art to the way Bing sang, just as there was an art to the way Fred Astaire danced. The art was to conceal the effort, to make it look as if anyone could

Best candidate for the title of America's greatest twentieth-century President,
F. D. Roosevelt, with all the confidence of an Ivy League background, proclaimed
his solidarity with the common man, pushed through the New Deal, and established
himself, through his Fireside Chats on the radio, as the ideal voice and conscience
of the USA. Crippled by polio, he expected, and got, a discreet silence from the press
on the subject. He was unfaithful to his famously intelligent and able wife Eleanor
but that was never mentioned either. FDR's immense stature was the starting point
for the build-up of media attention on the Presidency which would eventually
ensure that nobody with his human failings could ever be elected again.

The United States Ambassador to Czechoslovakia photographed fifty years earlier, when she was the most famous young person on Earth – Shirley Temple. All the standard horror stories were told about a pushy mother and a brutal studio that kept casting taller actors around her so she would stay looking small, but the really unsettling truth was that she was just very talented and professional, remembering her lines, hitting the marks, dancing the steps and flashing a searchlight smile long after all the surrounding adults had started begging for mercy.

do it. The microphone helped. Earlier popular singers such as Rudy Vallee had resorted to the megaphone, but by now the microphone had become sensitive enough for Bing to commune with it. He could sing 'Boo-boo-boo' to it as if it were a child's ear. The result was intimacy, the aural version of the close-up. So Bing was already a big star before he even got into the movies. His ears stuck out, but they didn't slow him down unless he faced into the wind. In his first film try-outs the studio bosses taped Bing's ears to his head. Gradually it was realized that it didn't matter if they sprang loose. Bing's extraordinary fame was solidly based on his being an ordinary guy.

The exaltation of the ordinary man looked like a threat to anyone who still believed that art was for the few. There were those in America who feared that their country might be overwhelmed with triviality. There were those in other countries who feared that the plague might be catching. As Hollywood movies spread American popular culture to the world, warning voices announced that although rule by dictatorship might be terrifying, America threatened something even worse: Shirley Temple.

Shirley Temple was a tremendous talent. She was America's biggest box office star for four years until puberty caught up with her. It had trouble catching her because the studio executives were understandably reluctant to let her grow up. There were rumours that they gave her reverse hormone injections, and surrounded her on the set with bigger and bigger furniture and taller and taller co-stars. Shirley Temple stories abounded. She was public property, so the whole world wanted to know everything about her private life. France was only one of the theoretically sophisticated countries that held a wince-along contest for Shirley Temple sing-alikes. All over the world, wherever thoughtful people were proud of their national culture, little Shirley Temple looked like a bigger menace than any of Hitler's towering blond storm troopers, who also enjoyed moving rhythmically to music, but at least didn't look winsome when they did it. But the thoughtful weren't being thoughtful enough. People wanted to see Shirley Temple movies out of their free choice, and to quarrel with that was to quarrel with democracy itself. Despite the damage she was supposedly inflicting on their higher brain centres, her audiences survived the Shirley Temple era. More remarkably, so did she. Not so long ago she was the well-respected *châtelaine* of the US Embassy in Prague. At the time of her early singing and dancing, however, the thoughtful people undoubtedly had a point when they wondered if this was what American culture added up to: a small but persistent noise.

In Europe those same thoughtful people soon realized that the fate Hitler had in mind for them was even more frightening than an American culture geared to the retarded adolescent. If they were lucky they headed for America. Famous refugees like Einstein got an early ticket. The less famous queued for visas. They were leaving terror behind them. But triviality still loomed ahead.

Already famous as the incomprehensible scientist whose theories about relativity nobody understood but everybody was impressed by, Einstein now became more famous still as America's unstoppable publicity machinery turned him into the nutty professor. He was perfect casting, right down to the accent. Once he understood he was stuck with the role, Einstein seemed to enjoy hamming it up. He poked his tongue out for the photographers, was content to pose sockless, had his hair cut on a biennial basis, and generally seemed to accept philosophically that a certain amount of flim-flam came with the territory. In an essay about his view of the world he stressed the importance of attaining a state of liberation from self. Liberation from socks was obviously part of it.

Other distinguished exiles from Europe adapted with varying degrees of discomfort to a new culture that seemed determined to rob them of their dignity. In his native Italy the great conductor Arturo Toscanini had been described as flamboyant. In America he was called Electric Whiskers. The man who had conducted some of Puccini's opening nights was not necessarily flattered by this description, but he got on with the job, turning the NBC Symphony Orchestra into a powerhouse for the propagation of classical music. Toscanini had set his face like flint against the blandishments of the dictators. Mussolini would dearly have liked the great conductor's allegiance. Hitler hoped that he would conduct at Bayreuth. Toscanini's refusal was as decisive as the scything arc of his baton. He unambiguously favoured democracy, whatever its vulgarities. Other eminent exiles were less certain. Towering representatives of Europe's uncompromising avant-garde landed up in the very place whose materialist iniquities they had spent their lives denouncing – Hollywood. Years went by before Stravinsky was finally granted the privilege of having his masterpiece *The Rite of Spring* cut up and used in Walt Disney's *Fantasia*. His admirers were appalled.

Stravinsky was less appalled, perhaps because he was grateful for the money. But that was as good as the famous European refugees ever felt about winding up in America. They had a phrase for it: *dankbar aber unglücklich*. Thankful but unhappy. They had come from cultivated countries that were no longer free into a free country that seemed to them uncultivated. Walt Disney was the symbol of all that they feared: a man made famous by a mouse, a duck and a shameless ability to exploit childish innocence on an industrial scale.

But not even Hollywood could replace all its flesh-and-blood screen stars with mice and ducks. Human beings were still thought to be a necessary evil. In the silent days the screen's leading men had glowed with charisma and flourished profiles that cut like swords. Now, as the Great Depression dragged on, the man in the street who was lucky not to be selling matches wanted to see someone not utterly unlike himself as the hero. It was a demand that the film studios were more than willing to supply, because less-than-outlandish film stars were thought easier to control. Ordinary-guy heroes rolled off the Hollywood production line one after the other.

Gary Cooper had the god-like features of an Easter Island statue. Off-screen his manners were highly sophisticated. From well-connected women he learned to move easily in café society. Some of the best photographers for the glossy magazines took some of their best photographs of Cooper. But on-screen the script said he was an ordinary guy and the ordinary guys in the audience believed him. He talked like a shy man made eloquent by a passion for justice. When Mr Deeds went to town he spoke for every man in America who felt victimized by economic disaster and political indifference. James Stewart was even shyer than Gary Cooper. Stewart took a long time to get the words out. To the man in the street who had the same trouble, here was his representative. When Mr Smith went to Washington he got the same reaction from the average Joe as Mr Deeds.

Henry Fonda was even shyer than James Stewart, even more passionate for justice than Gary Cooper. Fonda never got the chance to play anyone evil until he was an old man. In his early years he was a bashful but unbudgeable pillar of integrity. That was what the lines said and that was how he said them. Towering even above all the other pillars of integrity was John Wayne. No film star did more to convince his own country and the world that the

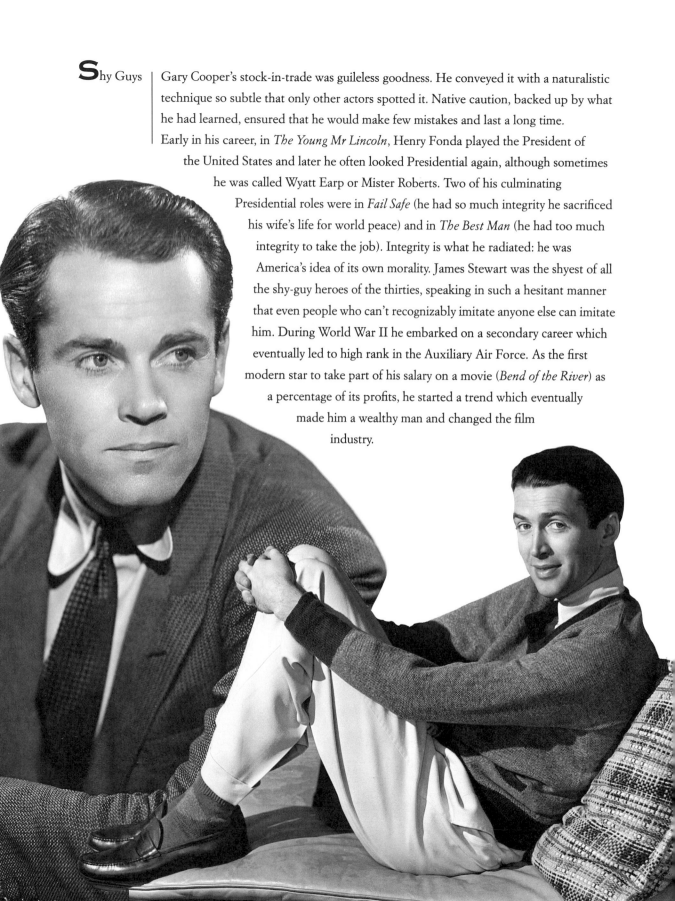

Shy Guys | Gary Cooper's stock-in-trade was guileless goodness. He conveyed it with a naturalistic technique so subtle that only other actors spotted it. Native caution, backed up by what he had learned, ensured that he would make few mistakes and last a long time. Early in his career, in *The Young Mr Lincoln*, Henry Fonda played the President of the United States and later he often looked Presidential again, although sometimes he was called Wyatt Earp or Mister Roberts. Two of his culminating Presidential roles were in *Fail Safe* (he had so much integrity he sacrificed his wife's life for world peace) and in *The Best Man* (he had too much integrity to take the job). Integrity is what he radiated: he was America's idea of its own morality. James Stewart was the shyest of all the shy-guy heroes of the thirties, speaking in such a hesitant manner that even people who can't recognizably imitate anyone else can imitate him. During World War II he embarked on a secondary career which eventually led to high rank in the Auxiliary Air Force. As the first modern star to take part of his salary on a movie (*Bend of the River*) as a percentage of its profits, he started a trend which eventually made him a wealthy man and changed the film industry.

ideal American male said no more than he could help, helped the helpless get justice, and was helpless himself when it came to women.

The new leading men all played the one character: the shy guy. There was the occasional aggressive exception but he had to play a psychopath. James Cagney was allowed to push a grapefruit into his girlfriend's face. Not surprisingly, in the light of later events, Cagney was Stalin's favourite screen star.

The only new leading man who was allowed to retain something of the old, rakish, pre-sound glamour was Errol Flynn – and he usually had to wear costume, in throwback movies that were essentially silent swashbucklers plus words. *Captain Blood* was one, *Robin Hood* was another, and Flynn was the same in both, trading in a frilled shirt for a fitted jerkin but retaining the same flagrant buckle for his swash. Flynn was born in Australia and thus blessed with the physical perfection common to Australian males. Off-screen he took full advantage of his appeal to women and got his name into the language with the phrase 'In like Flynn'. But on-screen his line of seduction was hampered by the lines in the script. Maid Marian's puzzlement about why Robin Hood should be so self-sacrificing was partly explicable by his apparent reluctance to make himself plain verbally. He was forever hopping on to a branch, leaping through an embrasure, or adopting any other posture that showed off his magnificent Australian leg.

The long-thighed and devilishly handsome Flynn was lost without his tights. Put him in a suit and he was gone. Put Clark Gable in a suit and he actually gained in authority. Gable was the ordinary man made majestic, except there was nothing threatening about him. He was friendly even when he frowned. Gable had a lot wrong with his personal appearance. He had the same ears problem as Bing Crosby and couldn't sing to make you forget it. His upper lip looked almost as weird with the moustache as it did without it. But it all added up to masculinity, especially when, as in the pioneering comedy *It Happened One Night*, he took the suit off, thus revealing the first pair of male nipples to hit the Hollywood screen outside Tarzan's well-worn patch of jungle. Gable was the ideal of the butch yet sensitive man in the street, a hero who could be safely worshipped without anyone getting the idea that a superman was leading little girls astray. In *Broadway Melody of 1938*, Judy Garland, still barely post-pubescent, could sing a song of adoration to him without anybody getting the wrong idea. She was merely making her obeisance to royalty. Gable was king of Hollywood. The publicity said so.

Hollywood, however, wasn't just a kingdom, it was also a business, and the king was on the payroll like everyone else. The male stars clocked on for work like the studio janitor. But in ten years they had come a long way. They had graduated from men of mystery to being all things to all men. For the women it was a bumpier transition. The biggest female film star of the lot didn't like the idea of losing her mystery, but the writing was on the wall. Under the influence of the New Deal, Hollywood had acquired confidence in the democratic process almost to the point of finding women of the people glamorous. With American democracy on its way in, the European *femme fatale* was on her way out. Garbo's art was at its peak. So she crowned her career with the hardest thing of all: comedy. *Ninotchka* was perfect, and she was perfect in it. Written and directed by gifted exiles, the film was a little piece of Europe transferred to America and kept safe. It was prophetically sad for the future. 'Bomps may fall,' said Garbo. 'Give us our moment.'

Soon she decided that she had had hers. Garbo quit while she was ahead. *Ninotchka* wasn't her last movie, but it was the way she wanted to be remembered. She went into self-imposed permanent obscurity with the media chasing her. They chased her all over the world. She never told them a thing. The most famous woman in the world had never conceded that fame imposed duties. During her career she never answered a fan letter, and after it was over she never answered a question. Twentieth-century fame was largely an American idea and in America private life was public property. Garbo was a European and she disagreed. Her day in the sun was over, but it was her business what happened at night.

The European women of mystery had been marginalized by the American women of the people. At the start of her career Joan Crawford didn't look like one of those. They made her up to look like Garbo. Gradually her own visual style asserted itself, starting with the make-up. She made aggressive use of lipstick, and looked as if she had been eating jam with a wooden spoon. Crawford emerged as a woman who fought for her own identity even when she was suffering from the torments of passion. She got the same-sized weekly mountain of fan letters as Garbo, but instead of ignoring them she answered every one of them personally. She was a pro. She put strength on screen. Though she was torn apart by anger and desire, you could see the steely resolve of the future director of the Pepsi Cola Corporation.

Joan Crawford was strong and Bette Davis was stronger. Here was a woman ready to stand up for her rights on the bare chest of a recumbent male. Davis was as strong off-screen as on. In real life she committed a crime which in Hollywood's eyes was worse than murder. She told the studio where it could put its bad scripts. The studio put her on suspension. She fought them in the courts. The world heard about her independent spirit. If Bette Davis had a point to make it was hard to miss. There was a characteristic moment in her movies when she shot the man who had done her wrong – or even the man who had done her right if she didn't agree.

These new strong women looked more like strong men than the men did. The shy American hero could only stutter helplessly while some triumphant goddess such as Katharine Hepburn ran rings around him. A whole new kind of movie was developed just to show this happening; it was called the screwball comedy. *Bringing Up Baby* was a prime example. Cary Grant dithered and Hepburn exulted, bursting with plans and ideas, all of them to his discomfiture except that he ended up happier than he could have managed on his own. For the sophisticated onlooker, the worrying aspect about America's ordinary-guy hero with integrity was that he always looked bewildered, as if his brain was his least developed muscle.

This was the period in which Ernest Hemingway, whose stories put a lot of emphasis on ordinary-guy heroes with integrity, became the most famous writer of the century, but it was for everything except writing. He killed at least one each of every animal in Africa. He caught at least one each of every big fish in the sea. Hemingway's lethal exploits were written up in the new picture magazines *Life* and *Look*, with photographs taken on the site of the massacre. Often Hemingway contributed the prose himself. Along with Scott Fitzgerald, he was one of the first serious writers to contribute to the men's magazine *Esquire*. Some critics began to doubt whether he could remain a serious writer at all if he adopted the life of the celebrity. But he himself had no doubts. It was his mission to establish the artist as a man's man. He was a walking advertisement for the life of action. He appeared in advertisements for beer. He gave advice on where the best food and wine were in which part of

Though excessive drink had already taken its toll, Ernest Hemingway in middle age remained a handsome man. One of the factors that made him the world's most famous writer was that he didn't look like a writer – he looked like a man of action, a view that he was keen to encourage. The dog was one of the few animals of any kind to survive an encounter with him. He shot everything and eventually himself.

The young Orson Welles weighed much less than the older one but bulked even larger – he was the boy genius of the American arts. After making the century's most famous radio programme, *The War of the Worlds*, he made the century's most famous 'art' movie, *Citizen Kane*. In the fifty years left to him before he made the world's most famous sherry commercial, he was rarely out of the news. 'There, but for the grace of God, goes God,' someone said of him, but in fact he had the saving grace of self-deprecation, although a gift for self-destruction went with it.

the world in what season of the year. He called it the straight dope. Hemingway knew the straight dope about everything, up to and including death. He didn't actually kill every bull in Spain, but he liked watching. He wrote a book about it. He used simple sentences. He said the simple life of the instincts was better than too much thought.

When Spain's own superman General Franco rebelled against the government, Hemingway attended the Spanish Civil War as if that were a bullfight too. He wrote a novel about it. He used simple sentences. The hero was a man who was simple and brave like his friend Gary Cooper. Hollywood didn't get around to making the movie until five years later, but the brave simplicity of the novel's hero was captured all too well. In the novel the hero and heroine had shared only a sleeping bag. In the movie Cooper and Ingrid Bergman shared some abominable pseudo-simple dialogue. It wasn't really Hemingway's fault. He hadn't really sold out. He had merely sold his novel. But there were those who said that fame was working in deadly combination with alcohol to corrode his talent.

For the sophisticated onlooker already worried about the European supermen, the American common man looked like the same threat from another direction. How could superior ability flourish in a culture ruled by a talking mouse? Orson Welles had ability so superior that he was famous almost from the cradle. He was the baby genius of the American theatre, his name known to all who cared for the arts. As a radio star he became nationally famous, his name known to many who didn't care for the arts at all but liked to be startled. He startled them too much with his dramatization of *The War of the Worlds*, which he made sound like a news report of an event that was actually happening. Welles forgot to say that the flying saucers from Mars were only fiction. Today Shirley MacLaine and thousands like her would be out in the backyard signalling the saucers in. But at the time a large part of the audience at home panicked. There were cases of heart failure and someone drove off a bridge. The *enfant terrible* back-pedalled, saying he never meant for anyone to be fooled. He said this not just to the press but to the newsreels. Everything he did was news. Though Welles was aware that a big audience would be unlikely to understand all of his subtleties he was not the sort of man who, having been shown a big stage, would willingly retreat to a smaller one. For his admirers, almost as daunting as the public's gullibility was the way the boy genius submitted to its judgment. It looked like the price of democracy.

Even in the British Royal Family, aloofness was brought down to earth when a strong American woman made an ordinary man out of the Prince of Wales. The consideration that he was a fairly ordinary man already – it could be kindly said of him that he had hidden shallows – would scarcely have been relevant if he had fulfilled his constitutional role. Unfortunately, or perhaps fortunately, he didn't. The Prince of Wales was already world-famous, even though his early accomplishments had not added up to much more than the successful wearing of clothes. But now he passed into legend. The Prince of Wales was all too briefly King Edward VIII before he quit, crownless, for the sake of Mrs Wallis Simpson, described by him, on national radio for all to hear, as 'the woman I love'. He passed into legend, and passed out the other side as the Duke of Windsor. He had put the role of the monarchy into question, but there was no question about his own role. He was an ex-monarch, self-condemned to an anti-climactic *après*-career as a non-paying international house guest.

One of the Windsors' first hosts was Hitler, for whom their admiration was unbounded. Hitler was delighted to see them. Here was further evidence that only the superman could cut the mustard in the new world order. Out-of-work kings were turning up to tell him he was marvellous. Hitler was in the position of a star actor who has too many famous people infesting his dressing room to shower him with praise. Britain's famous ex-Prime Minister Lloyd George, no mean seducer of the masses himself, dropped in for a drink. One of the famous Mitford girls, Unity, was so in love with Hitler that she shot herself during a spasm of ecstasy. Nobody in history had had this much publicity before and he started to believe it. He was infallible. If a fact contradicted his prejudices, it was the fact's fault.

When the black American athlete Jesse Owens won four gold medals at the Berlin Olympics, Hitler went home early and listened to his new set of *Siegfried* 78s, but failed to conclude that his theory about inferior races might have something wrong with it. Later on, the black American world heavyweight boxing Champion Joe Louis beat the Aryan ears off the racially pure German hope Max Schmeling. Americans of whatever colour were proud of their world champion, but Hitler didn't get it. He thought the Americans were so far gone they needed a sub-species to do their fighting for them.

Hitler was confident that America was a decadent culture and would do nothing while

At one time the Prince of Wales, briefly King Edward VIII, later the Duke of Windsor, always a talking point, he was the glass of fashion and the mould of form until he met an American woman who fatally wanted to blend her destiny with his without realizing that if that happened his destiny would disappear in a puff of smoke. Embarrassingly welcome in Nazi Germany, they sat out World War II in Bermuda before settling down to a long twilight trying on clothes in Paris and playing bridge in Palm Beach.

he cleaned up the even more decadent Europeans. He was vague about his next career move after that, but a strong hint was provided by what he told his mistress Eva Braun. The German public never got to hear about her except by rumour. Hitler assured her that things would soon be very different. He promised her that one day he would make her the biggest star in Hollywood. Home movies shot at Hitler's hidey-hole in Bavaria suggested that Adolf and Eva were a great screwball comedy team in the making.

Hitler *seemed* infallible, and at that time the look of the thing was everything. Fame was persuasive. A leader's image went unquestioned, even if he had manufactured it himself. If it had been wished upon him by the accident of his personal appearance, it was even more likely to be taken for reality. Neville Chamberlain was Prime Minister of Britain. It wasn't his fault that he looked like a walrus in search of a mate. In reality he was an able administrator whose bitter experience of World War I had made him passionately committed to avoiding a second. But he didn't *sound* passionate. He sounded as if he vaguely hoped that his keeper might throw him a fish. Too much of a gentleman to realize that Hitler wasn't, Chamberlain pursued an appeasement policy based on the fatal notion that Hitler's promises meant something. Chamberlain's most famous moment came after the Munich Conference when he flew home with Hitler's signature on a peace note that might as well have been a dinner menu.

The old-style European leaders were being acted off the stage by Hitler. He had them buffaloed. They were taking the image for the reality. Waiting in the wings, another superman was impressed with Hitler's performance. Joseph Stalin had already killed so many innocent people that not even Hitler would ever catch up. But Stalin was the most famous man in the Soviet Union, a title for which he had no competition apart from Lenin, who was safely dead. Through his monopoly of publicity, Stalin hailed himself as a political, artistic and military genius, fountain of all wisdom and father of his people. His people were in no position to disagree.

More remarkable was that people abroad agreed too. Once again George Bernard Shaw was loud in his acclaim for a dictator's powers of decision. Nor was Shaw the only great thinker with a soft spot for a strong man. Generally only the crackpots admired Hitler, but there were some sane fans of Mussolini and almost everyone with progressive opinions thought that Stalin's social experiment was worth the cost, especially since they weren't paying it themselves. More importantly, the strong men admired each other.

Hitler and Mussolini were a mutual admiration society, like two film stars basking in each other's glory, talking about making a movie together – hey, let's do it, I'll tell my people to contact your people. Hitler's invasion of western Europe started as a military onslaught and turned into a PR operation – the aggressive marketing of his image. Mussolini couldn't bear to be part of the supporting programme. He wanted to be in the main feature, so he went to war as well.

Stalin applauded warmly from the wings. For the moment Franco hung back, but how long would he be content to remain merely the biggest man in Spain? Unless they started fighting among themselves, it looked as if the supermen were due to run the world. Each supreme being had made himself famous for the one supreme quality: leadership. That his people might be following him only because they had no realistic alternative was a possibility that the leader tended to discount. Fame changed reality even for the man who possessed it. Hitler, in particular, grew more and more convinced as time went on that a master race was destined to follow where he led. The evidence was before his eyes. He had started to forget that he was the author of the show that was carrying him away. It failed to occur to him that there might be a more experienced showman with a better script and more convincing, because less histrionic, props: a bowler hat, a cigar and two extended fingers that meant victory viewed from one direction and rude defiance viewed from the other.

TWIN PEARL-HANDLED GUNS
1939–1945

For thousands of years before the twentieth century, history was just what famous people did. For the first forty years of the twentieth century fame had been setting up a history of its own, separate from the real one. A lot of famous people didn't do anything really historic except get famous, usually in America. But for two eventful years after the outbreak of World War II in Europe, it was like old times. History was back in Europe where it belonged, and the people making it were more famous than the Americans. They were running their own show again. The Americans were out of it.

In private, Winston Churchill was saying that unless America came into the war the jig was up. But for the nation he led and for the empire that his nation still controlled, the thing that mattered was what he said in public, and how he said it. Churchill's oratory was practically all that Britain had to fight with. The wings of the Few were lifted by his rhetorical flair. Few of the Few got famous at the time. The fame was all Churchill's. His nation and the free world were inspired by what was really an act – but it was a real act. He was really like that. He had been training for this part all his life. His only role was to lead the English-speaking peoples in a great crisis. If the great crisis had never come he would have remained an erratic figure fulminating at the edge of the stage, only occasionally called to the centre, sent back again after saying too much.

The hour had come when he was the only man to match it. There were plenty of people around him who had better judgment. That was what told them he was their only hope. He could act the part. Without his gift for dramatizing himself he would never have rallied his country at the last ditch. But if the machinery of twentieth-century fame had not been so highly developed, he might have failed to get his message out. The message was himself. The camera carried it to the people. After he made his great speeches in the House of Commons, he made them again on the radio. Rumours have persisted to this day that some of the radio broadcasts were made for him by an actor. It wouldn't have mattered, because

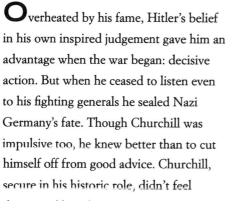

Overheated by his fame, Hitler's belief in his own inspired judgement gave him an advantage when the war began: decisive action. But when he ceased to listen even to his fighting generals he sealed Nazi Germany's fate. Though Churchill was impulsive too, he knew better than to cut himself off from good advice. Churchill, secure in his historic role, didn't feel threatened by other people's talent. Hitler did.

The greatest modern Englishman with only some of his carefully established kit of parts on display: the cigar, the bowler and the V-sign. Other props were a nautical cap and the 'siren suit', a sort of prototype Pete Townshend one-piece overalls outfit. People with good reason to distrust Churchill's judgement still trusted him to lead the nation when there was a single clear object in view: survival. They knew that only a role player could inspire.

what counted was those phrases ground out in that voice. If a mimic was imitating it, then it amounted to the same thing. Churchill was probably imitating it himself. He worked on his image: the siren suit, the cigar, the V-sign and the growl. He sounded the way he looked, like a bulldog. For just long enough, he united Britons of all classes in the belief that they were a bulldog breed. With the Continent fully occupied by a triumphant hostile power, the natural thing for the British to do would have been to give in. But they did the unnatural thing and fought on.

World War II had been a script by Hitler until Churchill started making up his own lines. As one actor to another, Hitler recognized Churchill as the embodiment of his country and was genuinely shocked by his refusal to see reason. The watching world couldn't help seeing the conflict in terms of personalities, because that was how the personalities saw it. Hitler *was* Germany. Mussolini *was* Italy. Stalin *was* Russia.

Stalin couldn't believe that Hitler would attack him. Capable of any degree of evil himself, he didn't underestimate Hitler's duplicity. But he didn't think Hitler would take such a risk. Having formed an opinion, Stalin thought it was a natural law. He was frightfully offended when Hitler invaded Russia. He took it personally. They all did. Hitler's new order had put the old world into such a state of disorder that a nation without someone to symbolize it was as good as lost. France *was* lost until one army officer who had escaped to England declared himself the embodiment of his nation's historic mission. Charles De Gaulle *was* France. He said so himself in the French language. But he had to say it on the BBC, and in France not many people were yet listening, not just because the Gestapo told them not to but because very few Frenchmen knew who he was. For the moment, the famous man they looked up to as the symbol of their national heritage was Marshal Pétain, a hero left over from the previous war, the war they didn't lose. For De Gaulle to replace Pétain in the national consciousness, he would have to appropriate the old man's prestige. It was a fame fight. De Gaulle had only a handful of soldiers and hardly any guns. He just had an idea. Free France. And he was it. *La France, c'est moi.* Visiting America, he sold himself as the symbol of his nation like a talking Eiffel Tower.

And America *was* Roosevelt, and Roosevelt was out of it. He wanted to get into it, but unlike the European men of destiny he had to listen to the voice of the people, and too

The man who knew most about the role of personal prestige in modern politics, Charles De Gaulle chose himself to embody the eternal spirit of his defeated nation. His next task was to get everyone else to agree. Some were never convinced – Roosevelt loathed him – but in the end he got what he wanted: free France, under his leadership, came back out of nowhere to establish itself as the leading post-war European power. Whether his country was well served in the long run is a moot point. Aided by his magnificent prose style – even his enemies conceded that he was one of the great modern French writers – he made himself so indispensable that he had to be brought back to solve crises, thus hindering the development of a governmental system that could function without a famous man at the centre.

When the war began in Europe, Judy Garland was still in the land of Oz. In her off-screen life she never reached it, being haunted always by her fame, which began too early, gave her no rest, and cruelly multiplied her humiliation when she failed to cope. Media obsession with her personal drama had the cumulative effect of leaving her tremendous gifts unreported – a sad case of fame burying the fact.

America had an old war of its own to rediscover. Appearing as Rhett Butler in *Gone with the Wind*, Clark Gable was already so famous that there was no other choice of male lead. But the instant world fame accruing to the role of Scarlett O'Hara was handed out as a gift to a woman only the British Empire had heard of – Laurence Olivier's wife Vivien Leigh.

many of them wanted no part of a foreign war. The isolationists were not necessarily cowards. One of the most prominent was the Lone Eagle himself, Charles Lindbergh. Lindbergh treasured his hard-won obscurity but gave it up again because he passionately believed that America should stay neutral. He pitted his fame as an independent spirit against Roosevelt's fame as the saviour of his country. It was another fame fight. In the late thirties Lindbergh had convinced himself that Europe was the business of the dictators, whose contemptuous attitude towards inferior breeds he had an unfortunate tendency to share. As a leading light in the America First movement, Lindbergh was effectively a weapon in Hitler's hands.

A world threatened with rule by supermen had all its suspicions about American frivolity confirmed. America was dreamland. Everywhere else, famous people made history. In America they made movies. In *The Wizard of Oz* Judy Garland sang about rainbows. It should have been Shirley Temple singing, but MGM wouldn't agree to the loan, so Judy Garland took her turn as the most famous girl in the world. She was as American as a talking mouse and wonderfully unconcerned with anything that was happening in real life. Was America coming to the world's rescue? Not yet. It was going somewhere else. It was off to see the Wizard.

While the outside world's supermen battled it out for the sake of the future, the Americans went in search of their own past. The most famous of their ordinary guys climbed out of his suit again, but not to put on a uniform. He put on a costume. Clark Gable was the only possible choice to play Rhett Butler, hero of the most famous popular novel of the period, *Gone with the Wind*. The period the novel was about was the American Civil War. The movie's advance publicity promised that it would be exactly like being there.

Gone with the Wind restaged an old war just at the very moment when the rest of the world was caught up in a new one. It was as if America was a world apart. The British actress Vivien Leigh was made world-famous overnight when she was given the part of Scarlett O'Hara. But the price she paid was to be Americanized. In the screen test she still sounded like a British actress doing a very good American accent. By the time the same scene reached the screen, she was as American as Judy Garland.

Gone with the Wind burned Atlanta in the special effects department the same year that

While still Crown Prince, in 1921 the future Emperor Hirohito toured Britain, where he was heavily influenced by the local Royal Family's style of dress. He never adopted King George V's plumed hat but he did copy the Prince of Wales's plus-fours. Debate about the Emperor's responsibility for starting Japan's share of World War II continues, but there can be no doubt about his responsibility for bringing it to an end. His intervention was decisive. Japan was rebuilt as a constitutional monarchy and the huge notoriety which had gathered around his name in wartime gradually dissipated, until by the time of his death there were few people in other countries who could pronounce it.

Hitler burned Rotterdam for real. It was as close to war as the Americans wanted to go. Hollywood's adventurous heroes were still exploring the world, but it was a fantastic world unconnected to the real one. A crisis to match Europe's was already building up in the Far East when America made its contribution to the understanding of the region's problems: *The Road to Singapore*, starring Bob Hope and Bing Crosby.

There was one great Hollywood star who knew that America couldn't ignore Hitler forever. He went into the attack with his most powerful weapon, ridicule. Charles Chaplin's impersonation of Hitler in *The Great Dictator* was hysterically accurate in every detail: the rant, the strut, the megalomania, the instantly inflatable eyes. Chaplin had even more experience of mass adulation than Hitler had, so he knew exactly what was going on in Der Fooey's mind. Chaplin gave it everything he had and it wasn't enough. Americans weren't going to be told by one European superman that they should go to war with another. If the ordinary guy was going to fight, he would have to find the reason in his own soul, like Rick, the sceptical expatriate American bar owner played by Humphrey Bogart in *Casablanca*. Off-screen, Bogart drank seriously but turned up for work on time like all the other Hollywood heroes. On-screen, he was the way American men saw themselves: making their own decisions. Rick, the on-screen Bogart, searched his soul to find out whether he should back the weak or stay aloof.

But the answer wasn't really there. The idea that the ordinary guy could decide his fate was an illusion. The issue of whether America should go to war was settled at Pearl Harbor by the Japanese, a previously anonymous people who were overnight required to personify themselves in the form of an arch-villain. He was the Emperor Hirohito, and no trapdoor had ever produced a less likely-looking demon king. The West had previously known little about Emperor Hirohito and vice versa, although on his one trip to England, in 1921 when he was still Crown Prince, he had met the then Prince of Wales and acquired from him a daring taste for plus-fours. The Emperor was so divine that not even his tailor was allowed to touch him, so whatever style of clothes he wore had to be fitted by eye. But they always had more charisma than he did. Hirohito was a fifteen-watt bulb. Yet the day after Pearl Harbor he was world-famous as Japan's all-conquering Emperor.

Prime Minister Hideki Tojo was elevated at the same moment to the role of the all-conquering Emperor's cold-blooded factotum. Better casting than the Emperor, Tojo had the advantage of actually looking as if he had evil thoughts on his mind. It was quite true: he had. His dream was of mass slavery for all Asian peoples, including his own. But he would have been demonized anyway, if only to make up for Hirohito's uncanny lack of any detectable spark. Since the Japanese power structure was hard to understand even for the Japanese, it was inevitable that the press in the Allied countries would groom Tojo as the more marketable monster.

The war was as big as the world, and far too complicated to follow unless it was dramatized into a battle between good and evil. Nazi Germany was a rich source of villainous leading characters, quite apart from Hitler himself. Before the war, Hermann Goering had played a complicated role as the second man in Germany. Hitler, who suffered from no vices except an overdeveloped taste for cream cakes and mass murder, had looked austere and dedicated beside Goering, a conspicuous consumer of fine wines and other people's property. Goering thought that he could divert attention from his weight problem by designing his own uniforms. It was a miscalculation on a massive scale. But Goering knew his way around a country estate, and this had fooled some of Europe's more clueless aristocrats into believing that despite his regrettable fondness for building concentration camps he might be a civilizing influence on Hitler. Now the gloves were off and Goering had emerged as a simple roly-poly figure of fun. British newsreels helped the gag along with specially edited Fatty Hermann compilations plus comic voice-over. When Goering's much-publicized Luftwaffe failed to beat the RAF, even the Germans got the joke. On the rare occasions when the Gestapo wasn't listening, ordinary Germans called Goering 'Meyer', ironically commemorating the moment when he had assured his countrymen that no enemy aircraft would ever appear over Germany, or else his name was Meyer.

Heinrich Himmler was no joke at all. Playing Tojo to Hitler's Hirohito, Himmler was cast as the cold-blooded horror who didn't even have the excuse of being crazy. Actually he was as crazy as a loon, ready to spend millions of scarce Deutschmarks on scholarly research to prove that the Japanese, like himself, were members of the Aryan race, seven-foot blue-eyed blonds in disguise. But Himmler rightly became world-famous for the aspect of his character that matched his personal appearance: he looked like a mild-mannered civil servant dedicated to his work. All the more sinister for looking so efficient, Himmler was *the* bad German.

And Field Marshal Erwin Rommel was the good German. Running rings around the British in the Western Desert, Rommel combined the unorthodox glamour of T. E. Lawrence with Baron von Richthofen's knack for looking chivalrous even while he was shooting at you. If Rommel had been fighting in Russia he might not have behaved so correctly. But the desert was blessedly short of innocent civilians and Rommel was fighting the right enemy, the British, who love a winner so long as it isn't them. They enjoyed coming second to him so much that orders had to be issued from on high making it an offence to credit him with paranormal powers. But nobody stopped calling him decent. It was a necessary belief. Somebody on the other side had to be good, or there was no hope for mankind.

And somebody on our side had to beat him. Faced with the uncomfortable challenge of admiring a winner of their own, the British came up with Bernard Law Montgomery. Like Rommel, Montgomery was good casting for a national hero. Montgomery had Churchill's positive attitude. But there were other British military commanders who had that and they didn't become famous. Montgomery also had Churchill's gift for belligerent showmanship, and that was what made the difference. He was so much the fierce warrior that he looked as if he was overdoing it even though there was a war on. The British will admire a superior man as long as he is eccentric, and professional soldiers didn't come more eccentric than Montgomery without being given sedatives. He was preposterous, but he was a tonic. Britain had a right to feel proud. For a long and crucial moment it had held the fort. Now the Americans were in but they were still getting organized, so Britain was saved from despair but still in the forefront of the battle. It was a time for glory.

Glory was the stock-in-trade of Britain's most glamorous aristocrat, Lord Louis Mountbatten, friend of the stars and the Navy's most dashing young commander. When his destroyer, the *Kelly*, was hit he brought her to harbour with her decks awash. Laurels were heaped on his noble, and noble-looking, head. It was one of a famous man's most famous moments. Mountbatten's admirer Noël Coward re-created it as an inspiring example of the very best type of staunchly nautical British movie, *In Which We Serve*. Celebrating Mountbatten's fame with a thinly disguised portrait, Coward increased his own fame as well. All the other

In a piece of symbolism that Dwight D. Eisenhower would probably have been unconscious of and Bernard Law Montgomery all too conscious, the Supreme Commander of the Allied Expeditionary Forces in Europe pins a medal on his ally and – the point of contention – subordinate. America had bought the war and Montgomery never really got over it. Like everybody else he liked Ike, but he bitterly resented Britain's second rank status. It affected his judgement. He pushed through the ill-fated Arnhem venture on the strength of his will alone, with no margin for error – a common failing among those famed for charismatic leadership. Eisenhower, who had no charisma, was more sensible: he was later drafted as President of the United States precisely because he was famous for not having let his prestige go to his head.

After the failure of the July Plot against Hitler's life, Hitler gave Rommel the option of committing suicide because he was too famous to hang. Regarded as a military genius even by his enemies, Rommel shared with his Japanese opposite number Admiral Yamamoto the unique distinction of being specifically targeted for assassination by Allied forces. In Yamamoto's case the attempt was successful. Rommel wasn't home.

Britain's equivalent to MacArthur as a glamour soldier was a Navy man,
Lord Louis Mountbatten. As a destroyer commander he was of questionable judgement,
but when his ship the *Kelly* was hit he bought her to port with dash and daring –
a ready-made seadog saga for his friend Noël Coward to turn into a famous film,
In Which We Serve. When raised to lead the British Empire's share of the war effort
in Asia, Mountbatten showed admirable leadership qualities, and after the war
his prestige was crucial in getting Britain safely out of India.
A lifetime's training in being famous helped.

actors on the prop ship were presenting a thinly disguised portrait of the ordinary fighting man. Coward/Mountbatten spent half the film addressing the chaps. On their behalf he waxed patriotic while they listened in tongue-tied awe, occasionally speaking but only when spoken to, and always in a strangled cockney accent. Coward's friend as he was the friend of everybody famous, Mountbatten was busy fighting. But when he couldn't visit the set he sent his relatives: the Royal Family. They approved of Coward because he was doing his bit, helping to buttress a benevolent Empire and a class system in which people knew their place even if they had their backs to the wall.

Mountbatten and a few other star officers of high rank might get famous but everybody else served. For them there was collective glory, in what Churchill called the war of the unknown soldier. The same went for the showbusiness stars, who were expected to do their bit through doing their act, giving a voice to the stiff upper lip. A man with a silly face who flailed a ukelele while singing pitiably uninspired songs, George Formby was popular at every level of the social scale up to and including the King and Queen. Here was convincing proof that the war had brought Britain's social classes together. A sceptic might have said that they were still separate, just packed tighter in the bomb shelter. But no one was listening to sceptics. The bombs and the entertainers were too loud.

Too loud and too piercing. Gracie Fields had a voice from downstairs that told upstairs people the British classes were all in the war together. When an upstairs voice delivered the same message to downstairs people it could sound more strained. Lieutenant Laurence Olivier of the Fleet Air Arm came home on leave to address a morale-raising rally in the Albert Hall. The startled audience heard their most famous actor as his natural self – a Plantagenet pretender with dialogue by someone who vaguely knew Shakespeare.

Famous actors pretending to be toffs were adding their highly polished voices to famous ukelele players pretending to be proletarians. In Britain's tangle of mutually irritating tones it was hard to sound natural. The only voice and face that were hard to place belonged to the woman who gave the British war effort its one true anthem: 'We'll Meet Again'. Vera Lynn's classless voice rang out to a nation which had never felt more like a family and an Empire which had never seemed more united. It was a culture that circled the world. Within it, in the warmth of what at least seemed like a new social cohesion brought about by the pressure of adversity, it was easy to believe that a Johnny-come-lately country like America was still a bit provincial despite its wealth and power.

After all, America's first military hero of the war led a retreat instead of an advance. With the Japanese triumphant all over South East Asia and the South Pacific, General Douglas MacArthur arrived in Australia to explain that his expulsion from the Philippines was only temporary. His explanation, however, sounded like a victory speech by the Emperor Nero. Even while he was still going backwards, MacArthur became world-famous for going backwards in style. His monumental hunger for publicity convinced the Australians that a British prima donna like Montgomery was a shrinking violet by comparison. To them, MacArthur sounded ridiculous. He should have sounded ridiculous to everyone. But with a war on, some of the old bets were off. Even in America, the land of celebrity, the celebrities had to take a step down and join the war effort along with everyone else. The political leaders and the top soldiers were the new stars, and the top soldiers could bask in glory only on the understanding that the war really belonged to the ordinary, anonymous foot-slogger, GI Joe, the American equivalent of Churchill's unknown soldier.

The Hollywood stars could hope only to serve, and if they were 4F, meaning medically unfit, then their best role was to raise morale. Bogart the tough guy wasn't allowed to fight. He wasn't 4F. He was simply too old. But he threw himself into the new task of flying off to meet the troops, coming home to say he had done it, and urging everyone to reach into their pockets. The Buy Bonds message was a way of raising morale and money at the same time. It was an honourable contribution. No longer on the road to fantastic destinations, Bing Crosby crooned for civilization. All the film stars did their bit, even if it was only to sling hash at the Hollywood Canteen. It was a new version of *noblesse oblige*: fame had its duties. Nor was it to be despised just because there was no getting out of it. Raising funds and fighting spirit was real work. It was even dangerous work. Clark Gable's beloved wife Carole Lombard was killed flying in bad weather to a bond rally.

But for Gable there could be only one course of action. Against the studio's wishes, he put his career on the line and joined up. Gable trained air-gunners for the Eighth Air Force based in England. Though he wasn't allowed over enemy territory as often as he would have liked, it was real duty. The event was duly publicized by the Air Force in the field and the studio at home, but the only line to take was that a mythical creature had resumed human proportions. The ordinary guy hero really was an ordinary guy after all. The actual man had replaced the legend.

James Stewart was another big star who put himself through the same reduction process, strengthening his links with reality but reducing his radiance for as long as he was away from the screen. The stars who joined the services – Douglas Fairbanks Junior went into the Navy – could be released to make movies deemed important to the war effort, but there was no avoiding a hiccup to their careers. David Niven, a British actor who was starting to make it big in Hollywood, would have made it bigger if he had not gone home and joined up. The pictures he made when on leave in England were strictly for Empire consumption. Doing his duty cost him the Hollywood starring roles that would have put him on top.

The same was true of Ronald Reagan. Much mockery was fated to be aroused by the fact that Reagan spent his war service making training films in Hollywood. But his eyesight was so poor there was no question of his seeing action. He could barely see anything. Nevertheless his war service exacted a true sacrifice. He was away from the big screen for long enough to lose all the momentum created by his most famous screen moment. As the amputee in *King's Row* he clutched at his missing legs and cried, 'Where's the rest of me?' It was the premature epitaph for the remainder of his screen career.

The stars who helped the war effort in any capacity were on unchallengeable moral ground. When they played soldiers in movies about the war, however, they inevitably courted scorn if they were obliged to look heroic. The unfortunate Errol Flynn, reproducing his erstwhile derring-do in a prop uniform, unwittingly detonated a diplomatic depth charge when he starred as the American who outwitted the Japanese army in Hollywood's most notorious war movie, *Objective Burma*. The trouble was that the war in Burma was fought mainly by Britain. The Hollywood film moguls had dismissed this as a side issue, but when the film was screened to British Empire troops there was a mass cry of derision. Australian troops who had previously been proud of the priapic Flynn's Antipodean origins were suddenly willing to concede that he really was an American after all.

Whether Japanese or German, the lethal enemy was a stranger, a hard target for specific hatred. The enemy obligingly provided some leading characters who lent themselves to

Humphrey Bogart, having served in World War I, was too old for World War II, but he did sterling work selling War Bonds and effectively symbolized America's entry into the conflict when he played, in *Casablanca*, the expatriate Rick, who had to overcome his own cynical reluctance before he came to the aid of civilization and Ingrid Bergman. In the movie he never actually says 'Play it again Sam' but we all insist on remembering that he does.

Errol Flynn was very keen to fight in World War II and it wasn't his fault that he was 4-F. Nor was it his fault that he was cast in the lead in *Objective Burma*. As an all-knowing American lecturing British troops on how to beat the Japanese, he aroused the derision of every non-American English speaker on Earth. But in the long run his fame as an irresistible off-screen seducer was undamaged.

brutal caricature. The enemy armies were easy to demonize because they behaved demonic-ally. But the loathing wasn't personal. There was nothing human to identify with and resent. The same was not true of the friendly ally. The Americans were familiar, all too familiar, and they were living too well – almost as if there wasn't a war on.

Despite all that the famous American stars could do to be one of the boys, there was always a new boy coming up to grab the glory and the girls. Frank Sinatra was 4F and not allowed to fight. Like all the other stars he did his bit for bond sales. But Sinatra's fame had little to do with the war. It had a lot to do with the rise of the teenager as a separate, powerfully vocal sub-group in modern consumer society. The female version of the teenager was called a bobbysoxer, and she thought Sinatra had been manufactured in heaven specifically to gratify her desires. The gratification expressed itself in wails of ecstasy that threatened to drown him out, but during lulls in the mass caterwauling he could still be heard crooning. Though it wasn't Sinatra's fault that the bobbysoxers went crazy about him, American servicemen overseas thought it was, and non-Americans everywhere had all their old fears confirmed that America was living in a world of its own.

If America *had* been living in a world of its own, American culture might have been easier to resist. But when the troops advanced, the culture advanced with them, marching to its own music – swing. Swing bands were like little armies with their own famous generals: Benny Goodman, Tommy Dorsey, Artie Shaw. They had spectacular skirmishers like the trumpeter Harry James and the frantic drummer Gene Krupa. The march was a dance but the swing musicians were always called invaders, especially if they were invading a friendly country.

Though it wasn't until after the war that James Stewart played Glenn Miller, for a Hollywood biopic *The Glenn Miller Story* was unusually exact in its evocation of period. The most famous swing bandleader had put his outfit into uniform and the result was conquest. Glenn Miller's music really did wow the British. His fame was a portent. The Americans brought a lavish, enjoyable way of life with them. The magnetic attraction of their popular culture was a kind of weapon. Miller himself vanished on the way into Europe, but there were more where he came from.

American culture was seductive, sometimes blatantly so. War production had pulled ordinary women into the factories, where it was conveniently discovered that their fragile femininity was more adaptable to handling machine tools than had previously been thought. Women stars did war work too, in a role that was then thought to be more inspiring than demeaning – the Pin-up Girl. Betty Grable was the most famous American woman in the war because she didn't appear just on the screen. She was pasted inside footlockers and painted on the sides of tanks and aircraft to raise the morale of men who hoped they might come home to a girl like her, or at any rate come home. Rita Hayworth was a greatly talented beauty who had shone as one of Fred Astaire's best partners. In normal circumstances she might have had a more fruitful career. The war transformed her into an upmarket dream girl. Though she married Orson Welles and starred in some interesting movies then and later, she never fully recovered from being such an object of desire. Personal insecurity always tempted her to agree that a woman so lusted after had no right to a brain.

But Katharine Hepburn could never be pinned down as a pin-up. She was too bright for that, and too confident. When America came into the war she had just starred in *The Philadelphia Story*, first on Broadway and then in the movie. She got the starring role because she had bought the rights to the script – a revolutionary step which opened up the possibility that a famous female film star could control her own career. An electrifying portrait of a woman who seemed to embody all the best possibilities of American prosperity and freedom, *The Philadelphia Story* was playing in Singapore on the day the British surrendered. Whether on screen or off, Hepburn proved herself the equal of any man. She was Spencer Tracy's partner in life as in art, but she was an equal partner. America was sending a powerful message to the world through its famous people. The message was that their country was so rich it had a way of life that the war hardly touched.

The message was rubbed in by the appointment of Dwight D. Eisenhower as Supreme Commander of the Allied Forces invading Europe. Ike had the knack of getting on with everybody. He could soothe ruffled feathers like Bing singing. He would have been easier to resent if he had struck Napoleonic attitudes like General MacArthur. But one of the most famous men in the world looked and spoke like a sales director for a vacuum cleaner company, and that was the point. The Americans had gone into the war business and out-organized everybody else. They had captured a global market. Even Eisenhower's name

Glenn Miller was only one of many famous American swing bandleaders – Tommy Dorsey, Artie Shaw and Benny Goodman were some of the others – but he acquired additional celebrity for his war service, when his band invaded Britain like a friendly army. It went on to invade Europe without him after he disappeared in a light aircraft on his way across the Channel. After the war James Stewart made Miller famous all over again in *The Glenn Miller Story*, and once again a Glenn Miller orchestra without Glenn Miller went on tour – a clear instance of Fame Lives On.

Raised in gentle circumstances on the East Coast of America, Katharine Hepburn was a prime example of what the Hollywood moguls were least confident about dealing with – a lady. They often miscast her, helping her to earn a place on the Box Office Poison list. She retaliated by taking control of her career to a degree unprecedented even by Garbo. Hepburn was the first actress to own and develop a major property – *The Philadelphia Story* – and make her stardom in it a condition of the studio's making it at all. The movie was a big hit and the studio executives made sure no woman could ever wield such power again for another forty years. Hepburn also succeeded in sharing a lifetime romance with Spencer Tracy without ever giving the gossips anything to go on. In her earlier, wilder years, she was one of the great loves in the life of Howard Hughes. At the controls of his seaplane she took off from New York's East River under a bridge, which would have been an impressive feat even for someone who knew how to fly.

sounded like a reminder to Hitler that the Americans didn't just have better dance music than the Germans. They had better Germans than the Germans.

Under Nazi pressure Marlene Dietrich had renounced her German citizenship but not her nationality. Meanwhile she had kept her German accent. Her presence in the forward areas was a sign that fame in America was a passport to everywhere. Taking the war over, the Americans had an endless supply of stars who turned out to be gum-chewing ordinary guys and gals at heart. On the other hand, their top soldiers seemed to be unbeatable at showbiz. When the Americans moved to centre stage in the Western theatre, their star warrior was General Patton. From North Africa to Sicily and on into Normandy, he moved in a blaze of publicity. On any objective assessment Patton's get-up of jodhpurs, high boots, lacquered helmet and twin pearl-handled guns made Mussolini's dress sense look understated. Some of Patton's opinions were likewise difficult to distinguish from Fascism. When he slapped a shell-shocked soldier in Sicily he had to be reminded on pain of dismissal that America was a democracy. Patton proved that Americans could be led by an entertainer as long as they thought he knew where he was going. Patton was going to Germany.

If Montgomery wasn't outshone by Patton as a strategist, he was certainly upstaged by him as a showman. It might have affected Monty's judgment. He was going to Germany too and tried to take a short cut, through Arnhem. The operation was a disaster that would never have been mounted in the first place if he had not staked his prestige on it, and it seems likely that he would not have done that if he had not felt outflanked and outranked – in a word, outyanked – by his upstart allies. The balance of world power had shifted to the Americans, and as an old Empire man Monty resented it for the rest of his career.

General de Gaulle was regarded by the Allied leaders as an even bigger prima donna than Montgomery, but in De Gaulle's own eyes he was justified. He was the symbol of his country, whose battered pride had to be restored. De Gaulle insisted on liberating Paris before the Americans. It almost happened, but one American beat him to it. If Ernest Hemingway's account can be believed – and his unsubstantiated account of anything has to be treated with caution – he exploited his status as a famous war correspondent to ignore the restrictions placed on regular troops, reached Paris before anybody else, and reconquered the Ritz Bar on behalf of civilization.

Famous people who had stayed on in Paris during the Nazi Occupation now emerged as Resistance heroes. One of them really was: Josephine Baker had risked her life and was awarded the Legion of Honour. The famous intellectuals Jean-Paul Sartre and Simone de Beauvoir were more dubious Resistance heroes because nobody else could establish that their Resistance group had ever done anything except meet. When Maurice Chevalier was accused of being a collaborator he said that although he had sung to audiences full of German officers he had been carrying out secret intelligence work. Picasso had sat out the Occupation in expensive restaurants eating black market food but now resumed his pre-war position as a champion of the oppressed proletariat. Jean Cocteau was a known collaborator but was forgiven because he was famous for his extreme sensitivity. Coco Chanel had at least been honest enough to live openly with a German general. After the Liberation there were suggestions that the famous *couturier* should be fitted with a *couture* noose. She prudently decamped to Switzerland until the fuss died down.

The supermen of the Axis powers had believed their own publicity and started a world war. Now the world was catching up with them. The comedown from unchallenged fame to human frailty was cruel. Mussolini had always been the most human of the supermen and the shock showed in his face. He was temporarily rescued from the collapse of Fascist Italy by his lifelong fan Hitler, whose divine status was also fraying at the edges, although he himself was the last to know. Hitler bankrolled Mussolini for one more try at starting another Fascist Italy. Returning to his country's northern area, which was still held by the German army against the Allied advance, Mussolini presided over the Republic of Salò, a grubby rump of a regime in which the Italian Fascists finally achieved the questionable distinction of behaving as disgustingly as the Nazis. Mussolini had run the full course from self-glorification to squalor. Caught by partisans, the disgraced *Duce* was hung up by the heels in Milan and would have seen his world turned upside down if there had been any life in his eyes.

Though things were looking bad for the men of destiny, Hitler still thought that his personality would decide the issue. He thought personalities made history. He was right about that, but continued to forget that everyone has a personality, not just the few geniuses chosen by fate. The group of young German officers and aristocrats who tried to bump him

General Douglas MacArthur's idea of an unselfconscious pose, complete with manfully clenched jaw. The corncob pipe, the cap heavy with gold braid and the dark glasses formed a carefully thought out kit of parts, set off by plain fatigues with no medal ribbons, because other generals had medals too.

In World War II MacArthur was only the co-commander of the Pacific campaign – Admiral Chester W. Nimitz had the same rank – but MacArthur got most of the publicity. His grandiloquence, however, came in handy for the job of rebuilding Japan after the war, and he would have ended his career in unquestioned glory if a lifetime's accumulated megalomania had not led him to forget that as a serving officer it was not his place to make policy. He wanted to end the Korean War by attacking China. President Truman reminded him he was mortal by summarily dismissing him from his post.

off were not untouched by the same delusion. When the plot misfired, it came out that they had enlisted Rommel as a replacement figurehead. If the trick had worked, Rommel's prestige would certainly have helped to keep the nation together, but only so that it could surrender unconditionally. As it happened, the matter was never put to the test. The bomb that the conspirators planted in Hitler's conference room went off all right but he survived the blast – final proof, in his eyes, that he was a chosen one. Wanting no further competition from Rommel's prestige, he gave Germany's favourite general the choice of either committing suicide or else seeing his family suffer – a medieval practice, called *Sippenhaft*, which the Gestapo had revived with conspicuous success. Rommel was lucky to be given the option. If he had been less famous Hitler would have hanged him with piano wire.

In his last days Hitler was a trembling wreck, yet still believed that his status as a man of destiny would deliver him a miracle – the death of Roosevelt. Roosevelt did die, but it didn't slow down the Allied advance by a single day. The Third Reich shrank to the size of one bunker under Berlin, where Hitler, determined to remain in charge of the production even though the budget had run out, arranged his own final curtain. Fanatical admirers later preferred to believe that he had gone on tour in Argentina. But fanatical admirers had suddenly grown few.

Hitler had been misled by the completeness of his own fame into thinking that Roosevelt, too, was the embodiment of his country. It was true, but it was only theatrically true. The drama of famous people just made things easier to understand. In the Allied countries, served by a comparatively free press, it was taken for granted that there was a difference between the great man's publicity and the real person, even if the great man showed signs of forgetting it himself.

MacArthur returned to the Philippines. He waded ashore several times to make sure the photographers got the shot. As the Australians had discovered in New Guinea, MacArthur didn't always remember to tell the press that his victories were gained with the assistance of other nations. MacArthur didn't always remember to mention other Americans. Mainly because of MacArthur's shameless self-publicizing, the belief persists to this day that he was the sole author of the island-hopping campaign that brought victory in the Pacific. In reality he was far outstripped for effectiveness by his naval opposite number, Admiral Chester W.

Nimitz. When it came to press relations, however, the General left the Admiral floating. MacArthur was the whole show. Whether his showmanship contributed as much to victory as his admirers thought was an open question, but there could be no doubt that it was decisive in the victory ceremony on board the battleship *Missouri* in Tokyo Bay. When he said, 'These proceedings are closed', he had all the authority of a ringmaster who owned the circus.

The defeated Japanese were hugely impressed by MacArthur, partly because he was so huge. He towered over Emperor Hirohito, but the discrepancy served them both. Jointly charged with the historic task of ensuring Japan's safe transition from a defeated militarist imperium to a modern democracy, MacArthur was the proconsul of the new world order and Hirohito was ready to play the humble representative of an old world order eager to take advice. The question of the Emperor's responsibility for starting the war never came up, partly because there was no doubt that he had played a decisive role in bringing it to an end. Tojo was not so lucky. Having attempted to commit suicide and failed, he was tried as a war criminal and sentenced to death. His fame fell through the trapdoor with him. There was no mileage left in being a superman. Hirohito stayed on as Emperor only on the understanding that he was no longer a divine being. He left all that to MacArthur.

Mountbatten was Britain's MacArthur, but his post-war role was very different. Mountbatten's prestige was employed not to extend British influence but to ease the way for its decline, by giving back India. His fame helped to make the process smooth. But it was the reality of ebbing power that had made it inevitable. Not even Gandhi's enormous renown was enough to ensure that the Empire would break up in the way that he wanted it to, without bloodshed. Some of the blood shed was his. Gandhi had been the symbol of India's struggle for independence from the British. From the British, at least, he had been safe from assassination. But with independence achieved, Gandhi went on to become the symbol of tolerance between India's own hostile religious sects. This time he wasn't safe at all. His name made him a target.

Famous characters had made the world conflict a drama that the worldwide audience could follow. The great events had called forth great men, or at least great names. But now their time was up. Churchill's unchallenged position, like the British Empire's unity, had

In his role as father of his people, Joseph Stalin made an international impact that distorted world politics for more than two decades, mainly because his admirers outside the Soviet Union didn't want to believe he had another role as murderer of his people. Many Russians including his own daughter tried to tell them, but his fame as a great leader was hard to counteract while he was still alive. In his last hours those few old colleagues who had survived his reign of terror gathered around his bedside to watch him choke.

been held together by the war. Peace was the downfall of both of them. His fine intelligence bamboozled by years of fame, Churchill had trouble understanding that the people who wanted only him to lead them in a war preferred anyone else now that it was over. His historic vision, however, was still working clearly. He went to America to warn one of the two remaining great powers about the intentions of the other. He would be a leader again, but only of a small country. This was his last world-famous moment, and he made it count. His 'Iron Curtain' speech was the formal recognition that the Western democracies were in a state of irreconcilable conflict with their former ally, the Soviet Union. It was no surprise: nothing except a mutual interest in suppressing Hitler could ever have brought about such an alliance in the first place. Churchill, though, as always, found the words that gave dramatic force to the obvious.

The only superman who had gone into the war and come out smiling on the other side, Stalin had effectively been Hitler's ally when the war started. Their non-aggression pact had given Hitler a free hand in Poland, and Stalin would have been happy to go on watching Nazi Germany chew up the democracies if Hitler had not made the supreme unforced error of invading Russia too. Having already stripped his own army of nearly all its best generals, Stalin was at first paralysed by the attack which he had always said would never come. When he rallied himself at last, his strategic gifts led his country to the verge of defeat. The Red Army turned the tide only after Stalin had been obliged to admit that some of his commanders might have almost as much military talent as himself. But he remained the infallible political genius. In the east European countries over-run by the advancing Red Army he made a point of turning out the few lights of liberty the Nazis had missed. Yet Stalin came out of the war looking more monumentally symbolic than ever, like a living statue. Since real information about what he was up to was even harder to get inside the Soviet Union than outside, it was no surprise that his countrymen worshipped him. But the admiration he attracted from otherwise well-informed people in the free world showed that, if a man was famous for employing supreme power in pursuit of an aim thought compatible with the collective good, evidence that he used it ruthlessly would only make him look more serious.

It was easier to say that the other superpower wasn't serious. With victory secured,

Hollywood fought the war all over again and made it look silly. Audie Murphy had been a real war hero, the only soldier to win the Congressional Medal of Honour twice. The movie moguls made a star of him, but put him in more westerns than war films because he didn't look enough like a soldier. They thought John Wayne *did* look like a soldier. Wayne had never fired a shot during the war, but now that the war was being refought he had thousands of shots fired at him. Luckily, on Hollywood's version of Iwo Jima the Japanese had been issued with bullets that bounced off tall actors running slowly. In cinemas all over the English-speaking world, ex-soldiers who had been through the real thing watched the fantasy with wonder, alarm, contempt and bitter laughter.

Meanwhile one of the real soldiers had hung up his uniform and was contemplating other forms of employment. The common man had conquered the world. Some were saying that the common man should run for President, but he wasn't saying it himself. Dwight D. Eisenhower disclaimed all ambitions for civilian office. He might genuinely not have wanted the limelight. But it wanted him. The fame he had gained in war for reconciling factions to a common end was too valuable to pass up for a peacetime political party in search of a candidate. The fame machinery which had been kept under some measure of control during the War of the Unknown Soldier was back on the loose. Worse than that, there was more of it. One of the new post-war domestic appliances, the one standing in the corner of the living room, was ready to unleash a new kind of American hero. He didn't sound much like an ordinary guy, nor was it immediately clear that he had come to save civilization. But when Liberace smiled at you only six feet from your sofa, you knew you weren't alone.

Nobody except his mother really loved Liberace but it turned out that
he had millions of mothers. Along with Lucy he was one of the stars of the
early fifties whose success suggested how big television would become.
Liberace offered class to people with no taste. Shrewd and sophisticated
himself, he knew exactly how to keep pushing his extravagance through new
frontiers, until finally his costumes filled a Las Vegas stage and had more sequins
than the city had lights. He didn't think of the line 'I cried all the way to
the bank' – it was a Hollywood chestnut. But he made it his by saying it to
the right person – a reporter looking for a quote.

CHAPTER FIVE

IN BONDAGE TO CYCLOPS

1945–1960

After World War II there were only two nations left that were still powerful, and only one of those was rich. America switched its huge production capacity from weapons to household appliances. Most of these appliances saved drudgery, so there could be no quarrel about their value. One of them, however, provided entertainment. It was the television set. At the touch of a button it produced a new kind of famous face.

Lucille Ball had been only a minor movie star. She wasn't remote or mysterious enough to make people dream. But television favoured the familiar and the cosy. At the age of forty, Lucy became the first major star of the new medium because she was very funny and she made people feel comfortable: lots of people. Thirty-five million of them in America alone. She was part of the furniture, a delightful featherhead who didn't challenge her audience to do anything except stop laughing. Off-screen, Lucille Ball was a clever businesswoman. With the help of her husband, Desi Arnaz, she turned her TV career into an empire. They recorded each episode on film in order to preserve it for future sales. In America, *Lucy* reruns went on forever and the same thing happened in other countries as they opened up their television systems, until eventually Lucy was on-screen somewhere in the world every minute of the day always. Lucy became so powerful she bought a movie studio, RKO. This was fame on a new scale. It wasn't employed, it did the employing. No movie star had power like that. When William Holden came on the show as a guest, the on-screen Lucy pretended to be in awe of him. The off-screen Lucy could have bought and sold him ten times.

Lucy was giving her fellow Americans a new kind of star they could live with, who lived with them. In the movies there had sometimes been sequences of films to exploit successful characters: Mickey Rooney as Andy Hardy was the most famous example. *The Lucy Show* went beyond that. It was a serial. She lived her life on-screen while the audience lived theirs watching. When she had a baby it was written into the episode. But her mind was written out. American TV seemed to assume that the mass audience couldn't take anything too complicated. They wanted it simple. They wanted it simple-minded. Enter, with his dental ivory flashing like the suddenly opened lid of one of his own highly polished pianos, Liberace.

Liberace left Lucy looking butch, but from the business angle he was just as hard-headed. Behind the coruscating cascade of notes he conjured from his keyboard was the background thump of an enormous cash register. In New York his TV show was on the air ten times a week. Millions of mothers out there wanted a son like him. Out of the ground came the cries of protest of classical composers as they spun in their graves. Liberace's smile never missed a beat, because television had joined him to a previously neglected audience of untold millions of people for whom kitsch was a step up. He knew how to play the subtle stuff, but he put in flashy runs instead. He created sonic cut-glass chandeliers to astonish people used to single lightbulbs.

His other inspiration was to dress himself and the set to match his music. A candelabra dripped wax on to his concert grand. There were furs on the floors, tapestries on the walls, and rings on his fingers like baroque knuckledusters. When he was called a vulgarian he delivered one of the most famous lines of the century: 'I cried all the way to the bank.' In a TV studio, monumental bad taste could be achieved on a relatively small budget. The road to Las Vegas and the world was open. The future stretched ahead, glittering with sequins. It was a kind of majesty. When he swanned along in his ermine-trimmed cape, he had only one rival.

The Queen topped him, but only just. Elizabeth II was launched in the same year as Liberace's first show, but in rather more dignified circumstances. Chosen by birth, she was going to be famous whatever she did. A lot, though, would depend on how she did it. The Coronation went off swimmingly, watched on television by the whole population of Britain, many of whom had bought a set just for the purpose. Later the colour newsreel was seen throughout the Commonwealth, but nothing could match that unique cocktail of grandeur and cosiness provided by squeezing the pageant into a box. Television had achieved its breakthrough in Britain in a dignified manner: intimate but not too intimate. A little corner of everyone's living room had become Westminster Abbey for the afternoon.

Arriving at the summit of Everest at roughly the same time as the crown arrived on the

Lucille Ball and her husband Desi Arnaz. Desi looked after the details of a business empire, Desilu, that revolved around Lucy, the first great star of American television and the pioneer of the future international television world, in which the Lucy show would be on the air somewhere every minute of every day, always. This feat was made possible by the team's prescience in recording the show on film, videotape having not yet been invented. Lucille Ball presented the next generation of militant feminists with a problem: on screen she was a helpless featherhead, while off screen she had the power of an industrialist. Which one was Lucy?

Queen's bare head, Edmund Hillary became the world's most famous New Zealander since Rutherford split the atom. His companion, Sherpa Tensing, became the only world-famous Nepalese outside Nepal. It seemed as if brave men were knocking themselves out to please the Queen. Roger Bannister ran a mile in under four minutes. Plenty of other athletes ran it faster later, but nobody else ran it that fast first. Continental countries didn't have miles, so his feat meant nothing there. But the Americans had miles. A Briton had done it before an American, and television brought the nation the news. Whether the medium could be trusted not to diminish the stature of Her Majesty's ministers was another question. Back in power for the last time near the end of a long and fruitful life, Sir Winston Churchill was persuaded to try out how he would go over on TV. Though he handled it quite well, Churchill decided that TV wasn't for him.

The Republican candidate for the Presidency of the United States, Dwight D. Eisenhower, didn't really handle TV well at all, but it was decided on his behalf that he had no choice except to appear. His powers of speech were no more impressive than they had been during the war. Either he strained to remember or he woodenly recited from cue cards. Eisenhower beat the Democrats because he had previously beaten the Germans, not because he was a great TV performer. What TV could do for the man with the right knack for instant sincerity was shown by his running mate, Richard Nixon, who defended himself against charges of bribery with a speech calculated to touch the heart, after a reassuring squeeze of the knee. The family dog Checkers was referred to, as if to own such an animal was a guarantee of probity. Nixon's oratory was like Liberace's piano playing. It was like being buried under an avalanche of pork fat. Dogs watching at home howled their derision, but an alarmingly large number of people were convinced.

Alarm turned to desperation when Senator Joseph McCarthy exploited the new media opportunities to turn his House Committee on UnAmerican Activities into a witch-hunt. Solid citizens knew that the real answer to Communism was democracy and that anti-Communism was a patent medicine, but they were afraid to say so. McCarthy's success scared America, and a scared America scared the world. McCarthy wasn't just getting away with it, he was getting bigger. When he attacked famous people, his own fame increased.

It was modern America's lowest moment. Accused of Leftist sympathies, Charlie Chaplin had no answer except that it was his constitutional right, and with McCarthy on the loose that wasn't enough. Forty years before, Chaplin had come to America to breathe free air. Now he was leaving it for the same reason. For the media it was a bigger story than any of his recent movies. A great man had found America uninhabitable. Another great man who found America uninhabitable in this period was Paul Robeson. A prodigious multi-talent who had as good a title to the role of all-round genius as Chaplin, Robeson was a linguist and a star athlete as well as a great singing actor. If *he* couldn't cure white Americans of racism, who could?

When he found that he couldn't, Robeson decided that the Communist countries had something to teach America about democracy. The Communist countries were delighted to hear this and gave him a well-organized reception. In countries with closed borders whose leadership held the monopoly of fame, ordinary citizens weren't encouraged to become famous without permission. But a visiting famous person lent prestige. His ears ringing with adulation, Robeson went back to America to discover that racist envy of his superior talents had been joined by McCarthyite condemnation of his Leftist inclinations. His passport was withdrawn. The great man was a prisoner in his own country. He reacted with some bitterness, as well he might have done.

It was easy to blame television for building McCarthy up. But it was also television that helped to bring him down. The TV journalist Ed Murrow did a programme on McCarthy that showed him for what he was – bluster, opportunism and petty larceny all wrapped up in one unlovely parcel. McCarthy was finished from that night. People found the courage to challenge him in committee. The camera worked for his opponents as well as it had worked for him. The centre of the action had moved to television.

This was the last thing that Hollywood wanted to hear. With its audience eroded by television at home, Hollywood fought back in the world market with everything it could think of. Released in the same year as the Queen got crowned, *The Robe* was filmed in Cinemascope, the first of many wide-screen processes designed to give the public something that television couldn't. Some of them were so wide that you couldn't get out of the auditorium without getting into the movie. *The Robe*, though, had something else besides a screen and a script that went on forever. It had Richard Burton. Previously

There were actresses more beautiful than Marilyn Monroe and almost every comedienne was funnier, but she was the one who dissolved the camera and appealed straight to the person in the cinema seat. The phrase 'The camera loved her' didn't really apply, because she had the knack, which amounted to a condition of soul, of behaving as if it didn't exist. There was just her, the people watching, and the other actors, whom she made better than they were by focussing all her attention on them. No one so self-obsessed was less narcissistic, to the point that her lack of self-esteem finally killed her. After her death her fame went on growing at every level from pin-up to intellectual icon. Arthur Miller, who was married to her, wrote an intrusive but fascinating play, *After the Fall*; Norman Mailer's *Marilyn* is an intermittently brilliant essay in dementia (his, not hers); and she appears as a character, the beautiful embodiment of inquisitive innocence, in a movie masterpiece, *Insignificance*, directed by Nicholas Roeg.

he had been Britain's most famous new stage actor. His co-star Jean Simmons had been a famous British film actress. Before the war, they might have been in two minds about going to Hollywood. Now Hollywood came to them. Riding in the new, big, four-engined silver airliners, Hollywood executives roamed the world to poach talent while it was still forming.

When Hollywood, with all the majesty of its blockbuster movie *The Pride and the Passion*, invaded Spain in 1956 – the same year that the Russians invaded Hungary – Cary Grant, who had himself originated in Britain, took a remarkable Spanish hostage. She was an Italian Spaniard, Sophia Loren, who was already well known in Italy before the siren call of world stardom lured her away. Hollywood wanted her because it was still haunted by the belief that only a foreign woman was capable of guilt-free sexuality. A well-built, healthy girl, Sophia looked as if she might give out affection as naturally as she took in pasta. America's own girls weren't like that.

All except one. Marilyn Monroe was Hollywood's home-based international ballistic sex bomb. Her impact was purely sensual. Nothing else was going on. Her every wiggle and pout seemed designed to attract men. The impact was doubled by her air of innocence, as if she might not quite realize what this instinctive mating display might lead to. The foreign women looked as if they were thinking about sex. Monroe looked as if it was something that might easily happen to her while she was thinking about something else. To call her vulnerable was a nice way of saying that she acted dumb. The studio made sure she had plenty of cleverly crafted dumb things to say. When she was asked what she slept in, she said, 'Chanel No. 5'. It was highly unlikely that she was the author of the line. The press quoted it as if it was hers because once she had said it, it was. Marketed like a new brand of warm, squishy merchandise off screen as well as on, Monroe was bigger as news than she was as art.

She did her best to make her private life a good story. Her marriage to the baseball hero Joe DiMaggio would have been made in heaven if God was a press agent. His masculinity, her femininity. His toughness, her tenderness. The story got better still when the marriage fell apart. One of the reasons it did so was media pressure, but the media didn't let up. Even bigger news than Monroe making it was Monroe blowing it, because the audience got a chance to cluck knowingly. The girl who had found success was in search of herself. She needed protection.

Her next protector was Arthur Miller, America's most prestigious playwright. Encouraged by Miller, Monroe started taking herself seriously as an actress. Actually there was no reason why she should ever have taken herself any other way except seriously. When not paralysed by fear she could play a part as if she was it, revealing all her vulnerability to the camera without seeming to be conscious of its presence, her whole attention on the other actors, helping to make them look natural too. Laurence Olivier, for example, may have hated every minute of working with her, but he never acted better on-screen than when starring opposite her in *The Prince and the Showgirl*. Though she was never the comic genius that some of her more perverse admirers claimed, talent wasn't what she was short of.

It was self-esteem. Not even Miller could help her find that. She was hell to live with and hell to work with, and that became the Monroe story even while she was at her most angelic on screen. In *Some Like it Hot* she looked like the happiest girl in the world. Even feminists who deplored her image of fluttering helplessness were unable to gainsay her air of joy as she banged out her theme tune, 'Running Wild', to a sleeping car full of all-female orchestra members, two of whom were Jack Lemmon and Tony Curtis in drag. There was a fascinating discrepancy between her on-screen radiance and her off-screen desperation. The girl with everything couldn't get it together. It was a story that suited everybody. People could enjoy watching her and then nod their heads wisely afterwards. Where would it all end? Only in America, said people abroad, pleased to be in on the story. In Hollywood they were in two minds. She might not be good for the movie she was in, which doubled its budget while the director waited for her to come out of her dressing room – or out of her coma. But she was good for the movies. Television couldn't give you Marilyn Monroe. From any angle, she wasn't Lucy.

Other countries tried to grow their own Marilyn Monroes, with varying success. France had the best try in the enticing form of Brigitte Bardot. Bardot looked even more provocative than Monroe and she also looked as if she knew what she was provoking. She drove older men mad by pouting at them, while giving young men what they weren't ready to appreciate. Her only drawback in the world fame stakes was that she pouted mainly in French. In

It was never fair to call Brigitte Bardot a French Marilyn Monroe. Monroe's appeal depended on being someone sex happened to, whereas Bardot made it happen to other people. Bardot was part of French sophistication even when she played the youngster on the verge of experience — she was a disingenuous *ingenue*.

broken English she could barely purse her lips, but at least that made it harder for the Americans to steal her.

Speaking French was the strongest weapon France had going for it in its diehard determination to protect itself from the ravages of American cultural imperialism. Britain's answer to Marilyn Monroe was Diana Dors and she was a sex bomb without a fuse, because Marilyn Monroe spoke English too, but on a bigger budget. Diana Dors made a few movies in Hollywood, but there wasn't room for her. She was stuck in England, where the movies she made reached no further than the British Empire, which was shrinking fast. So she was famous only on the home market and that was shrinking too. TV was booming and British movies were up against it. There was no money to waste on frivolity. Diana Dors gave the game away. Men might be fooled by her uncomplicated busty exuberance, but any woman needed only one look to know that she was up half the night helping to sew her own costumes.

Running short of heroic stature, Britain looked for it in the past. Only now, ten years too late, did the British war hero emerge in his full mythical glory. The film was *The Dam Busters* and the ace bomber pilot was Wing Commander Guy Gibson, DSO, DFC, GDE – Grimly Determined Expression. During the war the real Guy Gibson had been as famous as a bomber pilot was allowed to get at a time when all the other bomber pilots were expected to die unsung. He had his moment of glory, but it faded away along with 50000 dead aircrew including him. For Gibson to become a national hero the war had to be already won and his countrymen had to be in search of a winner. Guy Gibson was reborn in the form of Richard Todd, an adept at the basic feature of the British post-war war movie, the hero's man-to-man communication with the chaps. Thrilling to the marrow his briefing room full of uniformed actors, Todd/Gibson's man-to-man communication skills were closely modelled on Laurence Olivier's tally-ho oratorical cadenzas in *Henry V*, but with the poetry taken out and the upper lip restored to a decent stiffness. Backed up by a couple of real Lancaster bombers and some patently unreal bursting dams, the trick worked. Guy Gibson didn't just become a national figurehead, he became Richard Todd, and Richard Todd got stuck with being Guy Gibson.

The same thing happened to the most famous Battle of Britain fighter pilot. In the heyday of the Few, Douglas Bader won what headlines he was allowed to have because he was fighting the double challenge of the Luftwaffe and his missing legs. Now he found a third challenge: Kenneth More's energetic acting as the hero displayed his skill at man-to-man communication with the chaps. More suffered, as always, from his delusion that the expression 'Ha-ha!' would convey spontaneous high spirits. Nevertheless he managed to encapsulate without too much embarrassment the post-war British war movie's almost religious belief that the national gift for understatement could be celebrated without running the risk of overstatement. So Douglas Bader didn't just become a national figurehead, he became Kenneth More, and Kenneth More became stuck with being Douglas Bader.

Driven back on themselves by Hollywood's international dominance, British films were looking very local. It was against long odds that they produced their one unarguable great star, recognizable in every country where English was spoken without an American accent: Alec Guinness. He could be anybody. He could do anything. Unremarkable of feature, remarkable for the plasticity of his personality, he was a truly protean actor. With him as the star, the Ealing comedies gave the British film industry the only period of real self-confidence that it was ever to enjoy. But Guinness couldn't undo the facts of economics. Finally Hollywood conquered even him, although he made it look as though he had conquered Hollywood. Everyone in the British Empire that was now turning into the British Commonwealth assumed that Alec Guinness was the star of *Bridge on the River Kwai*. But he wasn't. William Holden had top billing. Lucille Ball's guest was Alec Guinness's host. Britain's most famous film star won his world fame in an American movie, as a supporting actor to an all-American star.

The most famous film director in the world was British, but he had moved to Hollywood before the war and made his name as an international Englishman with his own empire. His name was Alfred Hitchcock, and apart from that of Cecil B. De Mille it was the only director's name that the general public could recognize. Along with his name, Hitchcock promoted his physical shape as a logo. He made brief personal appearances in all of his films. He made his leading ladies famous just by choosing them. He liked to think that he created them, although in the case of his most famous leading lady he had to admit that she had a lot going for her to start with.

Alfred Hitchcock put his heroines on a pedestal so that he could scrutinize their behaviour under pressure. Though he was fond of granting fame to unknown actresses, Ingrid Bergman and Grace Kelly were both famous before they starred for him. With him, though, they acquired extra prestige for being in the only Hollywood entertainment films consistently taken seriously by sophisticates abroad, simply because they were directed by Hitchcock. The only director apart from Cecil B. De Mille recognizable to the general public, Hitchcock turned his name into a brand name and his bulbous physical shape into a logo. To journalists, any kind of suspense is Hitchcockian.

Grace Kelly finally and forever cured Hollywood of its inferiority complex about European sophistication. Born with a whole silver dinner service in her mouth, she had class to burn. From *Rear Window* and the other movies in the choice handful she starred in for Hitchcock, the steel billionaire's darling daughter emerged as an ice-cool WASP princess with fires raging beneath. Grace Kelly seemed to have taken to acting as a not entirely unboring alternative to just standing around being worshipped while her income discreetly piled up somewhere in the background. She sent a sexual message on handmade paper. The message reached men all over the world.

The millions of us that she jilted were bound to admit that Prince Rainier of Monaco had what it took to win the prize. Spreads in the photo magazines drove home the point that even Hollywood stardom was small-time compared to being a proper European-style princess. In fact Monaco was only a petite principality. It needed her to help fill its own casino and the world's imagination. For her, being Princess Grace was a role she could grow old in. It was the perfect conquest, in which the conquered embraces the conqueror. But it would never have happened without her fame, and only Hollywood fame was powerful enough to work the trick. Though it was a love match – what man wasn't in love with Grace Kelly? – it didn't hurt Rainier's little amusement park of a principality to acquire a big draw. Her patrician manners were just a bonus. Except in those countries whose borders were lined with barbed wire, the world was turning into a celebrity playground. Enter the American playboy.

His name was Hugh M. Hefner and he leaped to fame as the Editor of *Playboy* magazine, a publication dedicated to the principle that the libido of the ordinary American male should be set free. To help further this end, Hefner filled his magazine with mammiferous American females. His budget was so low that he could scarcely afford to airbrush the razor nicks off the nudes, but the enterprise took off when one of the women stretched across the slick layout turned out to be the woman the American male had already drooled over in the movies when she had scarcely anything on.

It was Marilyn Monroe, and this time she had nothing on at all. Hefner became a publishing tycoon overnight. But he wasn't just a publisher. He was a philosopher. At his Playboy Mansion in Chicago he lived between dusk and dawn, in conditions which would

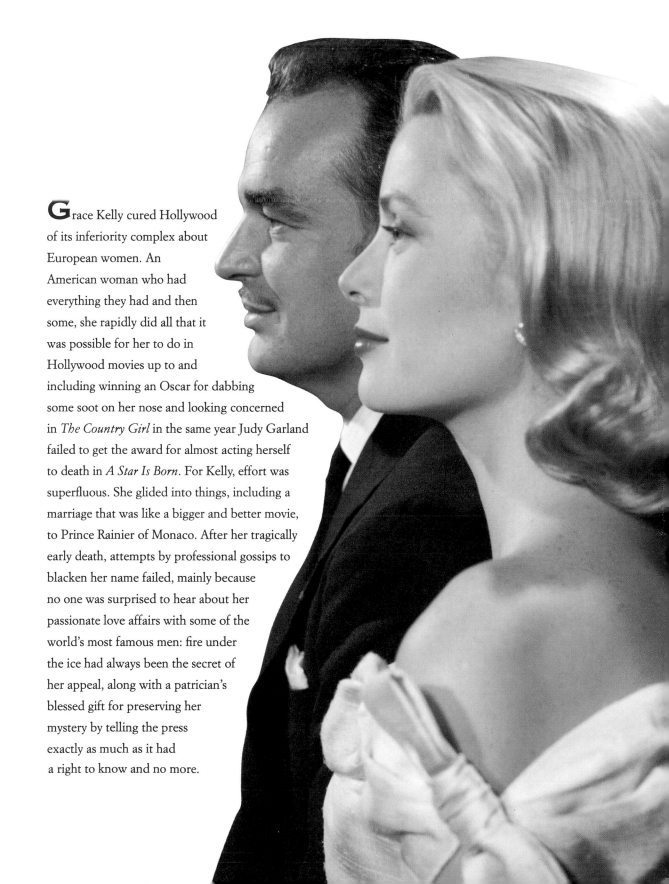

Grace Kelly cured Hollywood of its inferiority complex about European women. An American woman who had everything they had and then some, she rapidly did all that it was possible for her to do in Hollywood movies up to and including winning an Oscar for dabbing some soot on her nose and looking concerned in *The Country Girl* in the same year Judy Garland failed to get the award for almost acting herself to death in *A Star Is Born*. For Kelly, effort was superfluous. She glided into things, including a marriage that was like a bigger and better movie, to Prince Rainier of Monaco. After her tragically early death, attempts by professional gossips to blacken her name failed, mainly because no one was surprised to hear about her passionate love affairs with some of the world's most famous men: fire under the ice had always been the secret of her appeal, along with a patrician's blessed gift for preserving her mystery by telling the press exactly as much as it had a right to know and no more.

In Hugh Hefner's early days, before his historic move to Los Angeles, the Playboy Mansion was situated in Chicago and featured an underground bar from which he could look into the swimming pool and pick out his next playmate, like a gourmet, or in his case a gourmand, choosing trout from a restaurant aquarium. Hefner won fame not just for erecting Hedonism into a philosophy – it had always been that – but for making it a duty, like Stoicism. Reading his magazine and following his lead, men honestly believed that they owed it to the world, and not just themselves, to fulfil their desires. Some tired of the chase but Hefner never gave up his quest to make his dreams real: to live in a dressing gown, have a freshly made hamburger on call twenty-four hour a day and try out every young woman in the world until he found one who offered complete physical satisfaction with no responsibility, while finding what he said profoundly true instead of mortally insulting.

have looked like a Roman orgy if it had been restaged by Walt Disney with a popcorn concession in the solarium. Hefner gave hedonism mass-market appeal by sanitizing it. He promoted self-indulgence as a form of self-discipline, like body-building. Poised elegantly in the midst of the action, Hefner pronounced on the *Playboy* attitude to existence. Sound equipment was waiting to capture every gritty inflection, cameras lurked to immortalize the merest flexing of his thoughtfully clenched jaw.

The *Playboy* philosophy drew much of its power from what it was reacting against. Doris Day was still a bigger star than Marilyn Monroe. Doris Day was energetic and sexless, a deadly combination which left a man nothing to do except contemplate marriage – usually the one he already had. In the phenomenally successful *Pillow Talk* she and Rock Hudson romped daringly, but it was all too evident that she was only pretending to romp, although at that time few outside the film business were aware that he was the one who was *really* pretending.

The *Playboy* philosophy drew further power from jazz, co-opting *en masse* its supposedly cool heroes. In reality, most of the jazz greats led haunted lives. Billie Holiday was famous as the sad, lyrical voice guaranteed never to sound like Doris Day. But Billie Holiday's lasting fame depended, as she did, on the drugs to which she eventually succumbed. Charlie Parker succumbed to drugs from the beginning. His fame was established when he played a key role in turning jazz from a joyful music anyone could follow into a teasing, tortured brain-puzzle you had to be hip to understand. His fame was sealed when he died of drugs. Early death was taken as a mark of seriousness, proof that the innovator had been a chosen one. Miles Davis avoided early death, but always looked disdainful enough to suggest that it might a better place to go to. For the public he was the new Louis Armstrong, the jazz man they had heard of. But he sounded nothing like the old one. He hated the audience and often faced away from it when playing. He was cool, he was hip, he was in another world – the one where the famous people lived.

Fame was becoming a separate country, spread all over the world, inhabited thinly only by those known by everybody but who knew only each other. King Farouk of Egypt was a useless potentate in the old style. A globular monument to self-indulgence, he had the standard appetites for nightclub food and the kind of women who pretended that they couldn't run faster than he could. Pre-war he might have pursued these scholarly interests in relative privacy. Now his dubious achievements were reported from day to day. He was all lit up and it took a lot of electricity.

Aly Khan was like his father the Aga Khan all over again, but the old Aga had been famous only for racehorses and an annual salary of his own weight in diamonds. Aly was famous for marrying Rita Hayworth. He was famous for succeeding with a lot of other women who were married to other men. He travelled between love affairs in a succession of fast cars. 'They call me a wop and a nigger,' he said, 'and I f—— their wives.'

Fast cars were part of the playboy pattern. Motor-racing had always attracted aristocrats with time on their hands. Now the gentlemen were outstripped for glamour by the players. Juan Manuel Fangio was a dirt-track racer from Argentina who emerged as a nerveless, enigmatic hero, five times Formula One champion of the world. Women unimpressed by their husbands' driving said, 'Who do you think you are, Fangio?'

In Britain they said, 'Who do you think you are, Stirling Moss?' He was a brilliant driver, he was handsome, and he wowed the girls all over the world, getting out there and giving them one for Britain. He was patriotic, but really he lived in two countries. One of them was the fame country and it was everywhere. They knew his name in places where they couldn't pronounce it. Stairleen Mawse. Whichever way you said it, his name spelt speed, a flashing smile, a hairy wrist engulfing a heavy gold watch.

Aristotle Onassis spelt self-made man in Greek. He had built his fortune as a war profiteer renting out rusty cargo ships flying dubious flags. But nobody cared about how he had made his money because he was so spectacular about the way he spent it. He was a shady character who loved the limelight. He drew famous people into his orbit by offering hospitality too lavish to resist. Winston Churchill had saved civilization. Onassis had only hustled a few billion fast drachmas. But Churchill came to stay on Onassis's yacht. The genuine lustre of his distinguished acquaintances fed the spurious glow of Ari's own fame. The question of whether fame was deserved or not was ceasing to matter.

Eva Peron came to fame as the wife of the most famous man in Argentina, Juan Peron, whose neo-Fascist regime was found so congenial by Nazi war criminals on the run that they settled down there and learned Spanish. On the international scene Evita's fame

The most famous operatic soprano of the century, Maria Callas, gave her heart to a man who had capitalized on the wartime shortage of merchant ships to build a fortune matched in size only by his vulgarity. Some said that the secret of their alliance lay in the *diva*'s insecurity: since the devoutly Philistine Onassis knew nothing about opera, he must love her for herself. A more likely explanation is that Onassis had the resources to offer a woman sanctuary when her fame outstripped her capacity to protect it: later on Callas was moved aside in favour of the widowed Jackie Kennedy. Onassis and Eva Peron went to bed together within seconds of meeting – a flagrant example of instant intimacy through mutual fame.

exceeded her husband's. The press didn't care that the money for her *couture* clothes had been earned by the sweat of the peasants she claimed to represent. What counted was her vitality, her glamour, and her easily told story as a woman of the people who had risen to world conquest. Evita toured Europe and laid them in the aisles. Onassis later gallantly revealed that he and Evita seduced each other within minutes of their first meeting. Mutual fame was better than an introduction: it was a sort of pre-established intimacy.

The international fame show recruited stars even if they didn't want to join. Especially if. Albert Schweitzer said goodbye to civilization and buried himself in the African jungle to run a leper colony at about the time that T. E. Lawrence was trying on his first Arab head-dress. Now Schweitzer was like the man who had built the better mousetrap. The world beat a path to his door. Schweitzer had built a better leper colony. That was the assumption, because that was the best story. There was plenty of learned opinion to say that Schweitzer's methods were out-of-date and that his colony was the place to catch leprosy for anyone who didn't have it already. But Schweitzer's fame as the man who gave up worldly success to be a saint was too big to kill. Schweitzer spelt self-denial.

The story was about the world knowing who you were even if only an expert could understand what you did. Picasso loved being that famous. Pundits serious about painting might carp about his weakness for publicity, but his supporters had an answer. He was the genius, so his paintings were automatically serious. He was also serious about money. Fame increased his market and put up his prices. Every American multi-millionaire had to have his Picasso, even if it was only a piece of pottery. Soon Picasso was a multi-millionaire too. If he had any trouble reconciling this with his pro-Communist opinions, living in the South of France allayed the pangs. Picasso had always claimed the great artist's right to live by his own rules. In occupied Paris during the war he had dined at the best black market restaurants while the Gestapo were rounding up some of his friends. Now he treated art like a business while the world media treated everything he touched as art. Hardly anyone could tell a real Picasso from a fake, but it didn't matter because the real Picasso was Picasso himself.

Picasso wouldn't go to Spain while Franco still lived, and Hemingway wasn't allowed to return because Franco hadn't forgotten what he'd written during the Spanish Civil War. But in 1959 the ban was lifted and Hemingway was back there to watch the bulls bite the

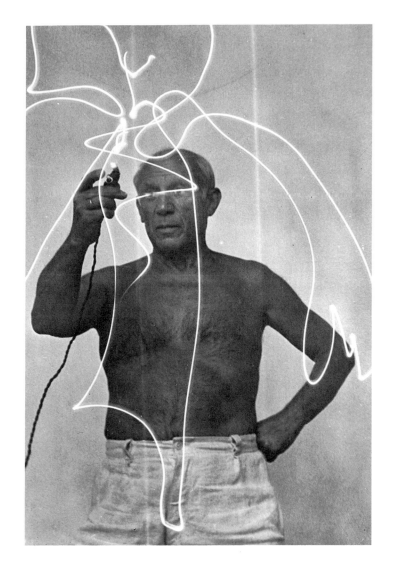

Famous throughout the century as the man who represented modern painting, Pablo Picasso was helped in the role by his unmatched technical facility. Even those critics who questioned his endless succession of new technical developments were unable to deny that he could draw as he pleased, getting it all in one line the way Mozart simply wrote it down. Picasso kept his mouth shut while his legend grew – the Garbo effect. In Nazi-occupied Paris during World War II he ate undisturbed in high-priced black market restaurants. After the war he backed proletarian causes while living the high life on the quiet: his chauffeured car was disguised with a taxi meter and the driver wore a beret. Picasso's women and children were brutally cast aside when they reminded him, by aging, that he was mortal too.

Frank Sinatra was always so identifiable that he didn't need his own name and was given others: The Voice, The Bony Baritone, etc. But Ol' Blue Eyes was a name he was never called except by the advertising man who thought it up as a logo for his second comeback. His first comeback was the most famous of the century, when he played Angelo Maggio in *From Here to Eternity*. In the movie *The Godfather* a singer rather like Sinatra gets a comeback role that sounds rather similar after the Mob puts a horse's head in a reluctant film mogul's bed. Sinatra's alleged Mob connections are part of his legend as a child of the gods possessed by the devil. All his qualities have their counter-qualities: an angelically gentle voice was matched from the beginning by short-fused behaviour, and a style-setting naturalistic acting talent was matched by a belligerent refusal to take his film career seriously. The general effect, that of a man determined to remain himself in spite of his own destiny, became identifiable as a cast of mind for which there was only one word: Sinatra.

dust. Or else he was out in the Gulf Stream killing fish. Or else he was in Africa killing animals again. Hemingway was always killing something. He called it an appetite for life. Hemingway lived in Key West, in Cuba, and in all the world's best hotels, always talking about the good wine and the good food and the good season. But he no longer wrote good books, although the Nobel Prize followed one of his worst, *The Old Man and the Sea*. He was an immortal while he was still alive. It no longer mattered what he wrote. He was just the Great Writer, the way Picasso was the Great Artist. Fame was a way of being that left doing far behind.

This was the time when Sinatra came back. After the war his career as both singer and actor had taken a dive that could have been the end of him. His role as Angelo Maggio in *From Here to Eternity* put him back on top as an actor. Sinatra's acting left the professionals looking wooden. This had to be the man himself, thin as a reed but indestructible as gristle. Sinatra doubled the impact of his comeback with a series of record albums that exploited the new $33\frac{1}{3}$ rpm long-playing format. They gave lonely would-be lovers everywhere a whole evening in the company of someone who seemed to share their solitude.

But beyond his renewed success as an actor and singer, there was his entirely new eminence as an international icon who was just Sinatra. His life took over as the main part of the story. Sinatra showed up all over the place with beautiful women, to some of whom he was married. He wouldn't talk to the press about any of them. When the press got nosy he got heavy. Swinging-lover stories made headlines.

Sinatra showed up in nightclubs with other men of Italian extraction who had never sung a note, even to a grand jury. When the press got nosy his bodyguards got heavy. Sinatra-hobnobs-with-the-Mob stories made more headlines. Sinatra just didn't seem to care about keeping his image smooth at the edges. He was too impatient to fool around with public relations – unless that was a public relations story too. He could have been the biggest star in Hollywood, but he didn't care much about that either. They had to get his performance on take one. He wasn't patient enough to stick around for take two. Except when he sang, he wouldn't dance for more than four bars to anyone else's tune. He wasn't interested in being someone else. He was himself. He was his own man. That was the message he sent to the world, as far as his voice could reach: that it wasn't what you did, it was how you did it. It was the way you were, or, if you weren't him, the way you wished you were: hip with a flip lip, no sweat, think sad but say it funny, getting the girl without trying.

The new Hollywood film star who really cared about acting was Marlon Brando. His initial impact made all previous film stars, even the most realistic ones like Sinatra, look as if they had been just saying their lines. Brando conveyed what was behind the lines. He conveyed emotion, whole complexes of emotions, bottomless wells of psychic disturbance. It was called the sub-text, and you knew that for Brando it meant more than the words because you couldn't always understand the words. Brando spoke English as if it were a foreign language he had acquired by sleep-teaching from a gramophone record running at the wrong speed. It only added to his appeal for alienated youth everywhere, because it sounded like the surly voice of social rebellion coming out of a classically beautiful face that you couldn't take your eyes off anyway, even if you didn't have to keep watching his lips to hear what he was saying. Brando's mumble was something only the movies could handle. Television wouldn't have stood for it. People would have kept adjusting the set.

Brando was a wild one off-screen as well. Every publicity still the studio got Brando to do cost them a week of persuasion. But the movie moguls stopped being angry when they discovered that Brando's reluctance to be publicized resulted in more publicity than they could ever have planned. The harder he rebelled, the easier they found it to market the rebellion. Feeling manipulated, he brooded darkly. His frustration was compounded by his lack of control over the movies he made. He could turn them down, but he couldn't set them up. No actor was that powerful. He had to play those big straight starring roles: Napoleon in *Desiree* (spit-curl on forehead), Sky Masterson in *Guys and Dolls* (hat on back of head). He proved that he could play them better than a brooding outcast might be expected to do. But a brooding outcast he always remained. Whatever he was up to on screen, the real drama was Brando versus Hollywood, Brando versus America, Brando versus the world.

The conflict was within. He was having a private crisis in public. He was more than a movie star, he was modern man. Modern men everywhere were influenced by him, some of them to their detriment. Far away in Tokyo, Japan's most famous writer, Yukio Mishima, had himself photographed as The Wild One, with a few slight changes to the wardrobe.

Rivalled only by Elvis Presley as the possessor of the most classically beautiful male face of modern times,
Marlon Brando had the acting ability to match. Able to convey layers of meaning
beneath the words – which indeed he often mumbled, changed or
left out altogether – he was a revolutionary artist but
Hollywood was a conservative institution, so a clash
was inevitable. It is a tribute to both sides that it was
so long drawn out. Brando had the chance to control
his career completely when he was given the finance
for *One Eyed Jacks*, but he blew it by going wildly
over budget. Back on salary, he sabotaged *Mutiny
on the Bounty* by asking for endless rewrites when it
was too late to fire him. After that he was
essentially a feature player,
although his fame
never went away.

Never in the history of twentieth-century fame did one actor become so famous for so few movies. James Dean was already dead in a car crash before his full impact had registered on screen, after which he went straight to immortality. Like Montgomery Clift (who might have attained the same pure legend if *his* car crash had killed him instead of merely disfiguring him) Dean had a feminine element to his mystique that helped him intrigue both sexes, although sceptics insisted that he didn't do much beyond wet his lips and pad the part by filling out every speech with pauses, sighs and Brando-like mumbles.

Only Hitler's long post-war period of residence in Argentina can be cited as a precedent for the widespread belief that Elvis Presley still lives and is willing, when the moon is in the right quarter, to go to bed with otherwise undistinguished housewives in selected motels scattered across the planet. Plastic surgeons in the United States do a staple trade in converting Elvis lookalikes to a condition steadily closer to the classical features of their idol. To trace the Elvis Presley cult back to its humble origins is like trying to walk on crutches down an escalator going up, but anyone old enough to have heard Elvis's first Sun records on the radio can remember what it was like to be blown twitching around the room like a leaf in a squall. It all started with the sheer joy of his rhythm.

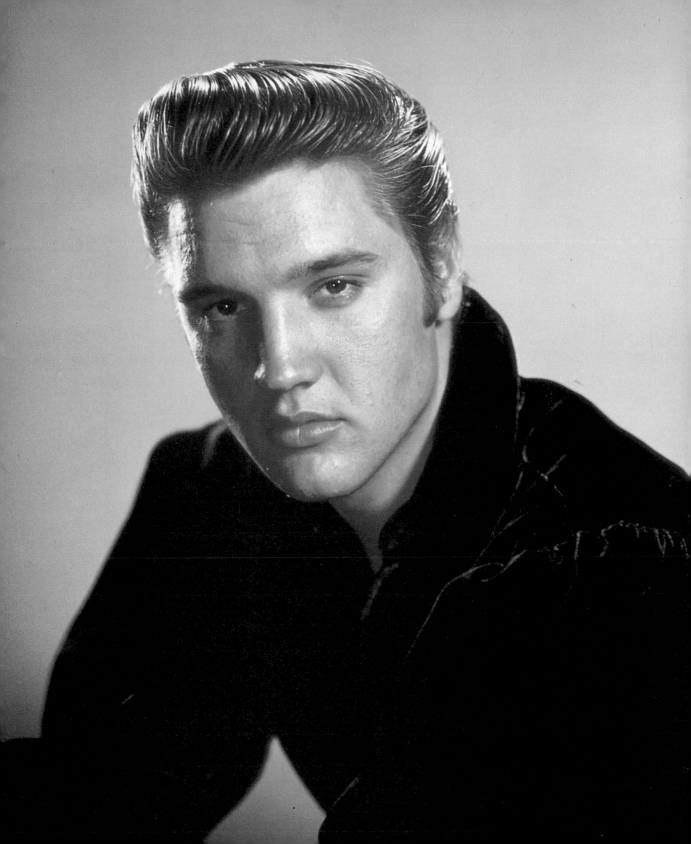

Where Brando had worn boots, cap, jeans, T-shirt and a leather jacket, Mishima, with traditional Japanese minimalism, reduced the costume to boots, cap and a daringly cut bikini.

Though he kept his clothes on, James Dean was a stronger challenger for Brando's crown as a champion rebel. In only his second major screen appearance, in *Rebel without a Cause*, he was such a brooding outcast he made Brando look like Danny Kaye. Dean took being young and inarticulate to new lengths. He took so long to get anything said that older people grew older still waiting for him to spit it out. There was a feminine quality to him which suggested that he had acquired some of his initial training as an actor by dressing up in his mom's clothes when she wasn't home. Actually Dean had started off in television with the capacity to deliver the line as written just like an ordinary actor. But Dean was an extraordinary actor and Hollywood knew it. He was given the mixed-up kid roles because the teenagers in the drive-ins in their father's cars wanted to see one of their own kind who dared to defy all those pettifogging grown-up conventional inhibitions such as bringing the car home instead of driving it off a cliff.

Somebody decided that Dean was the ideal person to give teenagers advice on safe driving. He filmed a public service announcement for television advising young people about the desirability of a sensible attitude on the road. Actually Dean's qualifications to talk about road safety were the same as a lemming's to talk about cliff-walking. If he had confined his speed mania to the racetrack he might have stayed in one piece. But he drove the same way on the public highway. Mistaking himself for an irresistible force, he went in search of an immovable object, terminating his film career just at the moment when his movies were making their impact on the worshipping young. The car crash stopped his body but his fame kept on going, free to fly into an unencumbered future while lonely young people pinned his picture to the wall, their own angel.

It was the Valentino option: frozen in motion before the lustre could tarnish. Some wag called his early death a good career move. But really it put him beyond a film career. He joined, on a permanent contract, a bigger production, the one in which an international cast of famous faces was up there all the time. He was the one who stayed young.

The young got their own music with Bill Haley and the Comets. Bill Haley wasn't young himself if you looked closely, but the audience was dancing too hard to keep him in focus. After decades on the road, Bill Haley was stunned to have suddenly got so far. His fame was abrupt and limited. There was no way to develop it. All he could do was rock around the clock again. The way was open for someone who actually looked the way the music made you feel: young, sexy, exciting, rebellious, dangerous enough to scare your mother yet strangely disturb her friends.

Elvis Presley came out of the South like an answer to a record executive's dream. He was a white black man. Elvis sounded no more comprehensible than Marlon Brando singing in the bath, but he had a face sculpted by Michelangelo crocked on moonshine and every move he made said sex. In his first few TV appearances he put all the moves in. Appalled at the prospect of America's youth being corrupted by Elvis's swivelling hips, the television executives panicked. By Elvis's tenth appearance they were shooting him strictly from the waist up.

Crosby and Sinatra had been hampered in their global reach by the dependence of their songs on the English language. Presley's universally incomprehensible slur went through language barriers like a silent movie. His records were released anywhere in the world where there were young people ready to love someone their parents hated. But Elvis wanted the parents too, or rather his manager did. Colonel Tom Parker's qualifications for running a big business were no more substantial than his military rank. He was a nickel-and-dime merchant whose idea of a smart move was to put an inflated price on the programmes sold at Elvis concerts. He knew nothing about the outside world and never allowed Elvis to go on tour outside America. But Colonel Parker did think big about maximizing his boy's home market. When Elvis's draft number came up, the teenage rebel went into the army without a murmur. He proved to be a model soldier, and his hitch of duty in Germany was a worldwide media sensation. A teenage idol was serving his country. He was a rebel *with* a cause. Elvis was practically part of US foreign policy, proof that if the Russians tried anything in Europe they wouldn't just be facing rockets, they would be up against rock singers as well.

Having proved himself a solid citizen, Elvis came home to find that he had increased his young audience while winning over their parents. His movie career boomed too. The

Colonel helped him pick the scripts. They might not have been the most brilliant movies in the world, but they were highly marketable because when Elvis had done enough talking he sang. It was all part of a plan for total merchandising of a product. If Colonel Parker had sent Elvis on tour abroad, the results would have been even more lucrative. But they were lucrative enough – revenue far beyond Elvis's capacity to spend, no matter what he ate, drank, wore, drove, married or injected. There had never been anything like the Elvis experience – in astrophysical terms he was a singularity – and there was no telling where it would lead. Music and movies had made a Memphis bumpkin into a planetary presence as inescapable as carbon dioxide. From those forced to admit through clenched teeth that the boy could have been worse, there were sighs of relief that there was no such thing as world television.

But domestic television was already having the effect of turning everyone who appeared on it into a performer. Vice President Nixon had become a household name like Lucy and Liberace. Russia's own front man, Nikita Khrushchev, had a big hit on television when he came to visit America. He had Mrs Khrushchev looming nearby to help him express his low opinion of Hollywood glamour. Khrushchev was a man who knew that, if he was going to bang his fist on the table to emphasize a point, he had better keep banging it until the camera got the shot. But Nixon came out on top in the famous Kitchen Debate in Moscow, when he went up against Khrushchev *mano a mano*, in a knock-down, drag-out contest in man-to-man communication. It was a double act like Dean Martin and Jerry Lewis or Abbott and Costello. Nobody remembered who said what. They only remembered that Nixon was starting to look like President Eisenhower's natural successor.

On screen, politics and showbusiness were merging. Behind the scenes they had merged. Men with career management as a career, men who dreamed dreams beyond the ken of Colonel Tom Parker, were already working on a fascinating proposition. If *Nixon* was Presidential material, what could be done by, what could be done *with*, a man with the right war record, the right wife, the right voice – the right face?

162

CHAPTER SIX

FLOAT LIKE A BUTTERFLY

1960-1969

The 1960s were the twentieth century's second most famous era after the 1920s. Really there is no such historical period as a decade. There are, however, times when a time becomes conscious of itself, partly because of the people who become famous. Until the 1960s, fame in the twentieth century progressed in step with the development of communications technology. But with all the technology in place including a television set in the kitchen, fame as a force didn't stop its forward march. Suddenly it broke into a run. The world's most advanced nation elected a President who looked like a film star.

John Fitzgerald Kennedy was as physically attractive as Marlon Brando and a lot easier to understand. He didn't look like any previous Presidential candidate. He looked more like people who were famous for other things: movies, upmarket sports, fooling around in the sun with beautiful women. The son of a rich Irish Catholic who had bribed and bullied his way to respectability, JFK had a background that could have worked against him. But his foreground worked for him. The children of the post-war baby boom were tipping the free world's demography towards youth. The Presidential candidate looked young. When he *was* young he was already a Presidential candidate, at any rate so far as his family was concerned. When his elder brother was killed in action during World War II JFK moved up to top slot. Making him famous was part of the plan. His own natural glamour was enhanced by strategy. JFK's PT-boat had been sunk in the Pacific and he had helped the crew survive. His heroism became part of the story.

So did his perfect wife, Jackie. JFK had the sexual energy of a male fiddler crab on a spring night, but that was left out of the story. The total picture was kept simple and polished like an airbrushed icon. In the famous television debate between Kennedy and Nixon, the experienced Nixon argued at least as well as his upstart opponent. Without the money his father poured into the campaign, Kennedy might never have drawn level with Nixon in the first place. But in the debate it was Kennedy's glamour that put him ahead by a hair's breadth, and the hair was on Nixon's jaw. The smart money said that Nixon lost the election by the whiskers he had neglected to shave.

The new President was no mere figurehead. He was able and energetic as well as attractive and spectacular. So there was almost no one at the time to question whether it was a good thing for the whole free world's combined media resources to churn out stories twenty-four hours a day about Kennedy's Washington being a new Camelot, with Jack as King Arthur and his brother Bobby an abrasive Sir Galahad. But if the euphoria threatened to encourage megalomania, there was always JFK's self-deprecating wit to prove that he had things in perspective. He made jokes about himself, and everyone else was allowed to as well. At a party packed with celebrities in Madison Square Garden Marilyn Monroe sang 'Happy Birthday' to him as if it were a torch song, celebrating his sex appeal along with hers.

All the jokes were flattering jokes. Few outside the family knew at the time that JFK was having an affair with Marilyn Monroe. But millions of people all over the world felt that they were in the family. Kennedy embodied a whole generation's idea of itself, so it went without saying that he was the whole American governmental system wrapped up in one person.

When Khrushchev planted nuclear-tipped missiles in Cuba and Kennedy demanded their removal, two famous men were deciding the fate of the world. The third famous man, Fidel Castro, wasn't even consulted. The missiles were in his country, but the real arena was the worldwide media. Kennedy persuaded Khrushchev to back down, and the result was interpreted as a triumph for Kennedy's character. Politics had become personalized to an unprecedented degree, at least partly because JFK was such an attractive person.

Part of the President's attraction was an attractive First Lady. Classy, cultivated, good at languages, Jackie Kennedy grew world-famous alongside her husband. The Western world was turning into a single TV network, and a large proportion of the Earth's total population tuned in to watch Jackie conducting a tour of the White House. Jack had the know-how, but Jackie had the *savoir faire*. She helped to make the world his oyster. When the Kennedys went to France to visit General De Gaulle, Jackie helped out with the diplomacy. Brought back from retirement as the only man who could keep France in one piece while it solved

America's ideal couple in their day of glory that seemed, from the moment when a rifle shot brought it to an end, further away than Arcadia. JFK never got over his grateful surprise at the availability of young women attracted to his fame. Jackie either knew about it but liked the compensation, or preferred not to know. The press said nothing and the world assumed that they were as happy as they were bright. Later on, with the media dictating the terms of entry to the upper levels of American politics, there was no further possibility of such a delusion, or of a President as brilliant as JFK.

the problem of what to do about Algeria, De Gaulle, like many of his most highly educated compatriots, distrusted American cultural imperialism and was determined to protect his country against it. But he couldn't deny that the Kennedys gave America a style and prestige to match its military and economic clout. Jackie wowed the locals by speaking their language.

Kennedy outsoared even Roosevelt, who had merely been the ideal President of the United States. Kennedy was President of an ideal United States. Kennedy reflected America's dream of itself back into its own eyes. He was dazzling. Only very old people who had read the Constitution dared to suggest that the star could bulk so large because the political system he dominated had grown weak. The founding fathers had intended that the President should be merely the first executive, not the whole show. But the founding fathers belonged to another century. This was the twentieth, and fame had done its work. The President was his country. Kennedy *was* America, and this side of the Berlin Wall it was an American world. With Jack and Jackie installed in the White House as a modern Ferdinand and Isabella without the PR problem, America's reverse conquest of the Old World continued.

America's cultural influence had become so seductive that countries which had fought a long rearguard action to retain their own identities showed signs of retreating into fantasy. Britain's fictional secret agent James Bond was an acknowledgment that most of Britain's factual spies had turned out to be working for the KGB. The actor Sean Connery became inextricably identified with the role. The script said that Britain had no independent power left. It was in partnership with the Americans. But Connery gave Bond a physical presence reflecting the influence that Britain would have liked to have, and the films clicked abroad because Britain actually had a new kind of influence – a new chic based on old brand names. Bond's easy expertise about upmarket consumer goods went down a storm with men uneasily aware that they might not be using the proper aftershave.

Britain had less power than it used to, but made more news. News was more interesting than power, and scandal was the most interesting news. Britain's Secretary for War, John Profumo, became involved with a svelte courtesan called Christine Keeler. Profumo was James Bond and Keeler was Pussy Galore. He was upper-class and she had only her looks. The suave Profumo found his Italian-sounding name permanently stuck on a very British style of media-maximized sex sensation.

Elizabeth Taylor and Richard Burton were a *folie à deux* in which only one of them was crazy – Burton. Taylor's fame worked for her because it didn't get in the way of what she was best at: being a celebrity. Burton, as the heir apparent to Laurence Olivier, was suspected by everyone including himself of having sacrificed his destiny on the altar of glamour. The film in which they acted out their relationship wasn't *Who's Afraid of Virginia Woolf?* – they had more fun in real life than that – but *Cleopatra*, in which Mark Antony, with an empire waiting for him, gave it all away so that he could climb into a bubble-bath with the head salesgirl from the perfume counter at Bloomingdale's.

167

London liked the idea of itself as Sin City. D. H. Lawrence had always been more famous than he would have been if some of his books hadn't been banned. When *Lady Chatterley's Lover* was finally unbanned he became very famous indeed. He had been the prophet of Britain's sexual liberation. Now it was here and he was one of its icons. Dead for thirty years, he was alive again. Britons were finding themselves so fascinating that the world was fascinated too. Peter Sellers could speak in a variety of British accents. He was a walking class system. Hollywood got interested, but couldn't quite figure out what to do with him until they made him a Frenchman. As the star of a whole series of films devoted to the adventures of the clumsy Inspector Clouseau, Sellers found himself world-famous – and trapped.

Richard Burton, Britain's wide-faced gift to the wide screen, starred as Mark Antony in America's mega-budget movie *Cleopatra*. America still needed Britons to play Romans. They had the right sort of accent: a kind of Latin you could understand. The movie went over the top in every way long before it was finished, and would have finished the studio if it had not been for the extra publicity earned by Burton and Taylor's off-screen love affair.

The affair wasn't really off-screen at all. It was a media event as over-the-top as the movie and with a budget that was only slightly smaller. Taylor was British-born but had grown up into the American Cleopatra in whose arms a succession of the world's illustrious men neglected their own destinies. Burton was just the latest. Taylor had won her first fame as a young star of outstanding beauty. As already mentioned, in *Father of the Bride* she had thrilled the world with her portrayal of the pretty girl on the verge of marriage. But one of the reasons she thrilled the world was that the world knew she had already been the bride of hotel heir Nicky Hilton. Later she went on to be the wife of the British film star Michael Wilding, whose noble profile included the kind of stiff upper lip needed to cope with the extent by which her fame outstripped his. She moved onward and upward to become the wife of the very famous American impresario Mike Todd. Not just their wedding but their entire brief marriage was a media event. After Todd's death in a plane crash Taylor took the famous singer Eddie Fisher away from his famous wife, Debbie Reynolds. That too became a media saga. All this before she got to Burton and fused her fame with his. They were a double act.

As an actress Taylor was limited to being only as good as the performance a director could extract from her. But she was protected against her limitations, and even against aging, by a media prominence that made her even more famous for being herself than for being an actress. Beyond being a film star, there was this new, bigger stardom of just being talked about all the time. It was like a chain reaction and Burton seemed glad to bathe in its glow, no matter what the cost. It cost him expensive presents, much of his credibility, and a fortune in alcohol.

The couple fought tempestuously in public, and the public paid to see them do the same on screen. *Who's Afraid of Virginia Woolf?*, though much touted at the time, was merely the least embarrassing of a whole string of films in which their clash of personalities was meant to be offset by a need for each other that they could not control. Burton was held up as an awful warning by those who said that British people in the arts should be offering the barbarous but powerful America a cultural example. To the two people involved with each other, however, there was only one country: the fame country, consisting mainly of luxury hotels linked by first-class flights. Burton lapped it up yet looked haunted. He was a very long way from Wales. He was a long way from anywhere, on the way to somewhere he didn't like.

Ernest Hemingway had been heading in the same direction for a long time and finally reached his destination. It was the ending he seemed to have been planning from the beginning. He had always been reckless with his life, as if he was living it to provide copy for journalists as well as material for his art. His legend took him over. His premature old age was brought on by his relentless pursuit of a young man's sensations. In Africa, on the hunt for the few remaining animals he had not already killed, he had a plane crash and woke up to read his own obituaries. His next move was to have another plane crash. When he recovered from that one he went fishing. He could never have enough of killing living things. Finally he did it to himself, with a shotgun. He had bagged his last trophy.

Marilyn Monroe also wrote her own last chapter: sadly close, in her case, to the first. The press had been carrying constant stories of the drugs she took to make her sleep. The press didn't yet know that she scarcely had time to sleep because she was having love affairs with both Jack and Bobby Kennedy. She was practically part of the Kennedy administration. It didn't help her. Her lack of self-confidence stemmed from childhood and no amount of success could cure it. When she was fired from *Something's Got to Give* no one was surprised. Her story was the one about the woman who couldn't cope with world fame. It could only have one ending. To supply it was practically her duty.

Not even the closed East was free from the influence of the glamorized West. The Russian ballet star Rudolph Nureyev defected to the West because at home he was artistically stifled and national fame wasn't enough. Forming a partnership with the Royal Ballet's *prima ballerina assoluta* Margot Fonteyn, Nureyev rose to the world fame that was his by right. It was good news for him and his art, but it was bad news for the Soviet Union. Any would-be world-famous citizen they produced was always likely to do a flit, unless his transport arrangements could be fixed so that he couldn't leave the country without having to come back. Such was the condition of the cosmonauts.

In a powerful counterstroke against the glamour of Kennedy's America, the Soviet Union sent a man into space. He was Yuri Gagarin, and he was the only cosmonaut able to shave accurately. Gagarin's cheeks were as smooth as Kennedy's, while most of his colleagues had a blue jaw like Nixon. If Gagarin had sported the usual Communist stubble the message would have been that they couldn't build an electric shaver. Gagarin's peachy jowls told the world that Soviet technology was as successful in the bathroom as on the launching pad.

Gagarin was a powerful weapon for the Russians. He showed what might be done if their leadership ever eased up on its monopoly of fame long enough to let the citizens have some. The watching world, however, was more inclined to welcome Gagarin as a world citizen than as a mere instrument of propaganda. Nevertheless it could not be denied that the Russians were one up. Kennedy's reaction to the Soviet space success was to forecast a feat beyond the dreams of Lindbergh: Destination Moon. He announced the intention of the United States to put a man on the moon within ten years. First the New Frontier and now the Final Frontier! Space. The Kennedy optimism would take mankind to the stars. What could go wrong?

What went wrong was that all the optimism was embodied in only one man, and the man had only one body. Everyone old enough to pronounce the word 'Dallas' remembers what he was doing that day, or pretends he does. JFK's early death became part of everyone else's

Yuri Gagarin was the Soviet Union's one sure-fire propaganda move of the early sixties, not just for getting into space but because he came back with such a nice face. His smooth cheeks and glowing smile distracted attention from the boiler-plate technology of the Soviet space effort, in which not even the scientists were safe. Gagarin himself died in a plane crash, but not before the whole world had learned to love him, and to hell with the propaganda.

Lee Harvey Oswald in an early attempt to avoid suspicion. Later he either shot President Kennedy on his own initiative, or fired some of the shots in a concerted attack, or else didn't do anything except take the fall – opinions vary, but since one man with a gun is easier to remember than a whole conspiracy, he is remembered for doing it whether he did it or not.

life. People got over the Lindbergh case: it happened to him. They never got over the death of Kennedy: it happened to them. They took it personally.

The assassination of the world-famous JFK made Lee Harvey Oswald world-famous too. There was no time to ask him if that was why he did it, *if* he did it. The assassination of the world-famous Lee Harvey Oswald made Jack Ruby world-famous too, but only for a few days. Conspiracy theories began about Kennedy's death, Oswald's death, Ruby's death. Somewhere inside the miasma of doubt, however, there was one unshakeable certainty: the Kennedy tragedy wasn't his alone. Everyone was involved.

JFK's fame lived on, pure, unsullied, brighter even than before. He had made a mistake backing the invasion of Cuba at the Bay of Pigs; he had okayed a build-up in Vietnam against CIA advice; and if his administration had gone on there would have been more mistakes, because all human beings, no matter how gifted, make them. But in his case the gap between the radiant film star and the fallible human being had not had time to show itself. Like a star's hand-print in concrete, JFK's myth was set in light. The TV natural was an all-media immortal.

In Britain, the Beatles became nationally famous and were held up as an awful warning that British youth had been corrupted by Elvis Presley. A few scattered adult voices held them up as a shining example of how British youth could now enjoy four home-grown Elvis Presleys with authentic regional accents. British youth said nothing because it was too busy screaming, especially the girls. The Beatles' songs were pop music of such insidious charm that even those who disapproved seemed to know the melodies and the words. The argument was really about whether young people deserved to have so much fun. Everybody had an opinion about the Beatles, and all the opinions could be summed up as a surge of pride that Britain had something of its very own to deplore – a uniquely British version of American popular music.

Somewhere in the middle of the noise, the Beatles scarcely had national identity on their minds. They already had a new nationality – fame, the borderless country that began in America but was growing all the time. Riding to the rescue of the shattered American dream came four new faces who had kept it intact in a foreign land. The Beatles arrived in America to the same reaction they had already aroused in Britain – an uproar from the audience that

The Beatles were so famous that even the people around them were names. Not just all teenagers but many of their mothers and fathers knew that Brian Epstein was the manager. With that scale and intensity of attention focussed on them, John, Paul, George and Ringo could have remained their sweet unspoiled selves only by a conscious effort. To their credit, they did what came naturally, which in the late sixties involved joining the search for the inner self. Inevitably they ended up with selves no more interesting than anybody else's but in the meanwhile they had turned out some of the best popular songs of the century. Since it is in the nature of pop groups to split – how long do men sharing a cell stay together without guards? – it was no surprise when they went their four separate ways, but John made a sad mistake in believing that because America knew most about celebrities he would be able to lead a normal life there. His murder took the last shine off twentieth-century fame. It remained alluring, but nobody thought it was pure.

drowned them out. Their young admirers were participating in their fame. As many admirers as could manage it participated by hurling themselves in front of the camera along with their heroes. Sceptics back at home were stunned that for once the British version of an American craze was going over big with the Yanks. But it was no mystery. The Beatles represented what their young American fans thought of as their own unspoiled, unsoiled, unsold souls. The Beatles weren't just products. They were people. They didn't sell themselves, they *were* themselves. The Beatles spoke a language that young Americans could understand, even if the accent was hard to figure out. It was the language of authenticity. The record industry might be marketing the authenticity, but they couldn't manufacture it. The artist had to have it.

The possibility that he might fake it obviously didn't arise in the Beatles' case. Bob Dylan's case was more of a problem. Going in the opposite direction to the Beatles, America's new troubadour toured Europe. Though he had changed his name from Robert Zimmerman and was open to charges that no one who wrote such fluent lyrics could possibly speak in so inarticulate a manner without practising in front of a mirror, he came over as even more authentic than the Beatles. Coming over, however, was an activity whose operational details seemed to concern him almost as much as his music. Did he really have difficulty in speaking plainly to the press, or was he just pretending to, so that they would pile on the speculation? Was he Garbo with a mouth organ?

Dylan's songs evoked a childhood of blue-collar poverty and hopping freights. Actually he had a middle-class background and the only freight he ever hopped was his mother's car to school. The roots he sang about going back to were long gone, but he seemed to believe that they might come again. It was a seductive message.

Dylan's audience discovered him. He wasn't wished on them. It was as if they had wished him into existence. He was their poet and balladeer, the lone voice who could sing a bit for the millions of lone voices who couldn't sing at all. On their behalf he transformed rebellion into protest. Rebellion had been for crazy mixed-up kids like James Dean. Protest said that society was mixed up. Dylan's audience was everyone who was young enough to believe that society was repressing their creative originality. The market was huge, and Dylan didn't have to accommodate to it. He could sing and play as he pleased. If you were young, or could pass for young in the dark, the popular music star was a new kind of hero even more seductive than the film star.

Meanwhile the man who started it all was marking time. Elvis Presley was marking time at the top, but the Beatles and Bob Dylan and all the other lone voices of questioning youth might have found it harder to grab the world's attention if Elvis and his handlers had realized that music was taking over from movies as the number one vehicle to project a star's personality. Elvis made three potboiler movies every year for the kind of audience that swooned with envy instead of nausea when they read about his pink Cadillac. He could have been more demanding but he would have had to be a different person, and Hollywood a different place. Rock stars could sing what they liked but film stars couldn't set up their own movies. Only one star was big enough even to try.

Marlon Brando, still Hollywood's number one brooding outcast, took his revenge on the Hollywood system he hated when it starred him as Fletcher Christian in the remake of *Mutiny on the Bounty*. Brando did a stunning job of almost getting an upper-class English accent right, playing the role as a brooding outcast who had been to Eton. But Brando's real brilliance went into sabotaging the movie's budget. Once the studio was committed to the voyage and it was too late to turn back, Brando demanded endless rewrites to make Fletcher Christian's part bigger than Captain Bligh's – an impossible requirement. Nor would Brando learn his lines when they were rewritten. The words had to be taped to the ship's rail. This explains why Fletcher Christian, when addressing his fellow officers of the *Bounty*, spends so much time apparently staring overboard.

Taking in less at the box office than the film cost to make, with all the distribution costs a dead loss, the studio ended up in the same shape as the *Bounty* – on the rocks. There were mutterings in the industry that no star, least of all Brando, would ever be given such power again. But the problem remained that the *Bounty* fiasco had made Brando more famous than ever. There would always be a movie that needed him even if he might wreck it. Brando seemed to enjoy the grief he was giving to the men in suits. When he ate, it was *their* weight problem. He could order a cheeseburger with fries and call it a challenge to the Establishment.

In Britain the Rolling Stones mounted their challenge to the Establishment by rising to

Carrying his whole instrumentation on his person, the early Bob Dylan had low
overheads. Not looking like part of the popular music industry was part of his appeal.
Everyone who could pick out three chords and sing through his nose could be just like
Dylan. Later on he went electric and forfeited some of his first following, but he gained
a huge extra audience of young people who were starting to like the idea – the central
paradox of the sixties' youth culture – of a social revolution operating on an industrial
scale. Dylan was the first rock star to suffer from a fan going through his garbage.
Later rock stars simply published it in book form.

prominence without cleaning up their act. Unlike the Beatles, the Stones were not cute, lovable mop-tops that even parents couldn't help feeling protective about. The mere appearance of the Stones' front man, Mick Jagger, was enough to make parents call the police. On the matter of drugs, Jagger paid no lip service to hypocrisy despite looking as if he could pay lip service to a locomotive.

The Stones were out to shock the Establishment, and the Establishment obliged by inviting them to explain themselves. Asked to participate in the newly developed electronic version of the Athenian symposium, the television discussion programme, the Bishop of Woolwich, the future Lord Rees-Mogg and other venerable religious figures strove to understand. Jagger, despite the irreversible effects of the costive mumble he had laboriously adopted to disguise his middle-class origins, strove to be understood. But finally there was no understanding because the whole impetus of the youth culture was based on rejecting the values of the established order so as to recover the concept of shared humanity. The problem of how someone could become famous for professing these things and yet somehow remain identified with his fellow members of the youth culture was left until later. The Stones were the incorruptible representatives of a non-conformist social movement, gurus of a new vision. Gurus of the old vision obliged by completely failing to understand the new message that making love was better than making war. American evangelist Billy Graham toured Britain and expected to stir outrage when he announced that he had seen young people blatantly making love in the open air. Christians who were shocked by the mass appeal of the rock stars were glad to hear Billy Graham reaffirming Christian values. But Billy Graham himself was more like a rock star than like Christ, who never rented a stadium or held a press conference. The distinction between the old-style holy-rollers and the new gurus was blurred by the requirement that both kinds of messenger needed coverage and the coverage became part of the message.

The division between idealistic youth and untrustworthy age would have remained more clear-cut if the new gurus had not gone in search of old gurus of their own. The Beatles' John Lennon had already shocked those who professed to be Christians by unwisely letting slip the perfectly true observation that the Beatles were more popular than Christ. Those who professed to be Christian were further shocked when the Beatles went chasing off after

A man being attacked by his own hand, Billy Graham was always confident that God would intervene. Commanding technical resources unknown to Jesus Christ, the Billy Graham crusade constantly toured the world's major cities, filling the stadium every night for a carefully calculated short run as it worked towards the big moment when those who wanted to have their lives changed were asked to Come Forward. Many of them did, and their lives *were* changed. The Billy Graham crusade went on somewhere else and left them behind.

an Eastern mystic called the Maharishi Mahesh Yogi, a hairball with a line of chat recognizable to experienced idealists of the previous generation as a perfectly standard bill of metaphysical goods.

Aided by his direct pipeline to the godhead, the Maharishi was able to tell his young acolytes that the secret of inner peace was to remain untroubled by outside events. Though there was no refuting this, when the holy person proved to have an appetite for fame far exceeding their own the Beatles went home disappointed. On the question of fame, the youth movement was in a dilemma disguised as meditation. They wanted to be individuals, but they were looking for leaders.

The Maharishi might never have proved disappointing if the Beatles hadn't gone to see him. Che Guevara had the advantage of remaining inaccessible. Born in Argentina, he helped Fidel Castro liberate Cuba from Batista and the Yankees. Put in charge of the new revolutionary Cuban economy, he proved his detachment from material things by running it into the ground. Prudently packed off by Fidel to help revolutionize Bolivia, he was ambushed and killed by the forces of reaction. From then on he could only be read about, and his true fame began.

Che, the complete romantic article, was the subject of an untold number of romantic articles. Writing about him became a stock-in-trade for everybody contributing to the youth culture's alternative press – thousands of low-budget publications, scattered worldwide, which added up to a powerful new mechanism for exalting a few individuals in the name of equality. Che's poster was pinned on the wall of every student who believed in a new kind of political order driven by thoughts of love and peace. It was never explained how any admirer of Che could accomplish this in a fully industrialized Western country when Che himself had been unable to organize anything more complicated than a small ambush. It was never explained because the question was never asked. Che's undoubted glamour was taken to be a virtue in itself. His beret was a halo. He was a kind of non-singing rock star.

An even more unlikely object of veneration for young Westerners seeking liberation was China's all-powerful ruler Mao Tse-tung. Yet there were very few readers of *Rolling Stone* anywhere in the world who could bring themselves to make a connection between Mao's absolute power over a thousand million people and the tendency for so many of them to meet an early death. Near the beginning of his career as the Chinese People's Republic's supreme source of all wisdom, Mao had staged the Great Leap Forward, a master plan designed to transform China's economy. In the process he killed more of his own people than Hitler and Stalin put together ever managed to kill of theirs. But since Mao held the monopoly of publicity, none of the blood showed. The world saw only the waving flags. Mao continued to build his unchallenged position as political genius, spiritual leader, philosopher and sporting hero. The wrap-up worked at least as well for export as it did for home consumption. It was assumed worldwide that the smiling guru was doing what he had to do to feed his people, and that if a few million of them should happen to starve it was only a mark of how serious the problem was.

In the 1960s Mao prepared a repeat performance of the Great Leap Forward. This time it was called the Cultural Revolution, and the main purgative element was composed of students who waved Mao's little red book while demanding punishment for anyone who had committed the crime of growing old and set in his ways – anyone, that is, except Mao. Western students liked the idea of Eastern students exercising so much power over their elders. It was a kind of rock concert, like Woodstock. They might have liked it less if they had seen the bodies, but once again all the world saw was the waving flags. In 1968, the year that the Cultural Revolution swept through China with full force, bringing death and misery to millions of innocent people, Mao was canonized in the West as a compassionate, all-embracing Buddha in a Beatles suit, his mere existence serving to prove that capitalist, imperialist America couldn't, shouldn't, have things all its own way.

Mao was especially admired by French intellectuals sold on the idea that all the world's young idealists could be united in a crusade against the US capitalist imperialists by a suitably sexy version of Communism. In Paris, Jean-Paul Sartre did most of his marching against America. He did little of it against Russia and none at all against China. Sartre was merely the most prominent French intellectual glad to acknowledge Maoist tendencies. But Sartre did it on a world scale. For the would-be serious young everywhere, he was a guru.

At the very moment when his much-admired Mao was taking steps to ensure that every Chinese equivalent of the French intellectual should have his spectacles trampled underfoot

If there is a question about whether Hitler or Stalin killed the greater number of innocent people, there can be no doubt that Mao Tse-tung killed more than either, yet his fame, both inside and outside China, was for being the guiding light of a necessary historic process. Information about the scale of his ruthlessness did little to alter opinion based on wish fulfilment. French intellectuals who regarded the USA as the cultural enemy were proud to call themselves Maoists even when Mao was persecuting his own intellectuals as a matter of principle. The irony reached its savage peak in the sixties, when the flower of Western youth pinned its hopes on Mao's China at the very moment that his Red Guards were dealing a blow to his country's social fabric from which it has never recovered – the Cultural Revolution.

by the Red Guards, Sartre attained international fame. He was seen as the profound existentialist soothsayer who was able to prove that the occasional apparent injustice in the East was merely part of an historic process, whereas the West was threatened by the infinitely more insidious evil of the American-style mass consumer society. He was calling America a force for evil at a time when many sincerely concerned Americans agreed with him. On campuses across the USA, students who wouldn't have been able to get past page one of *Being and Nothingness* knew his name. It was on page one of the newspapers.

One good reason for admiring Mao's Little Red Book was that it didn't sound like John Wayne's dialogue. Helping to confuse the issue in Vietnam, Wayne made a film called *The Green Berets* explaining how the Americans had come on a crusade to save a small South East Asian country from destruction. In reality, the crusade was somewhat compromised by the scale of the destruction the Americans were causing on their own account, but Wayne wasn't concerned with reflecting reality. He was out to change it, by swaying the world audience with the force of his example. He was using his fame as the strolling, drawling straight-shooter. In fact this reputation was based entirely on movie appearances and when not on screen he was just another actor who collected paintings and wives, but in his own mind he was what he was famous for and he could safely assume that his fans felt the same way.

All the world's young liberals thought that *The Green Berets* was the funniest movie in the world. But it was the favourite movie of the young Lieutenant Calley, who became temporarily but frighteningly famous himself when he stood revealed as the instigator of the My Lai Massacre. A whole village full of innocent people got wiped out by a John Wayne fan. For those who needed telling, this was compelling evidence that upright, uptight, right-wing America was in serious trouble with its role models.

Muhammad Ali never needed telling. He preferred to do all the talking himself. A cute lip was part of his equipment, along with good looks, a cheetah's reflexes, a bomb in each hand and a brazen personality. In an earlier incarnation Muhammad Ali had been Cassius Clay, winner of the Golden Gloves and an Olympic gold medal, a World Heavyweight Champion of unmatched speed and grace, the latest and most electrifying example of a youngster fighting his way out of the ghetto to an unlimited future. He was young, gifted and black – a famous phrase at the time, although he could easily say better things himself. His description of his own prowess – 'Float like a butterfly, sting like a bee' – proved that whatever he lacked as a poet it wasn't verbal inventiveness. The world warmed to him. He brightened life. But as with so many previous black celebrities, global acceptance didn't guarantee a fair shake at home. Though Cassius Clay seemed made for the American dream, his response to a whole society rigged against the black man was to join a different society altogether: Islam. Hence the change of name. And his response to being drafted for Vietnam was not to go. His change of name hadn't changed his fame, which he put on the line to influence events.

Vietnam wasn't Ali's war and it wasn't Martin Luther King's war either. He had another war on his hands. Before Martin Luther King, there had already been a movement towards black civil rights in the United States. With Martin Luther King, the movement became a man. He made non-violence a principle and put his life on the line to back it up. His weapon was to have no weapons: the way of Gandhi, moral authority. Any rewards he had coming for his leadership he accepted on behalf of those he led. One of the rewards was the Nobel Prize for Peace which for once was bestowed on someone who had unambiguously devoted his life to that very thing.

He also accepted most of the danger. Having made himself the centre of the story, he had made himself the focus of hostility. But there was no way out of it. Without TV coverage there was no chance of the movement creating pressure in Washington, and television wanted the story to have a hero. King won a victory in the South. But when the battle moved north he was up against a more ruthless opponent even than FBI chief J. Edgar Hoover, who had merely bugged his bed. He was up against his own fame which expanded with his territory.

King was a moving target. The target grew larger when he came out against the Vietnam war. King condemned the social conditions which sent black young men to do more than their share of dying for a country in which they did less than their share of living. That made him the embodiment of the Civil Rights movement. It was really no surprise, least of all to King himself, when someone decided that if the body could be hit in the head the whole thing would die. The news of King's assassination circled the Earth and darkened

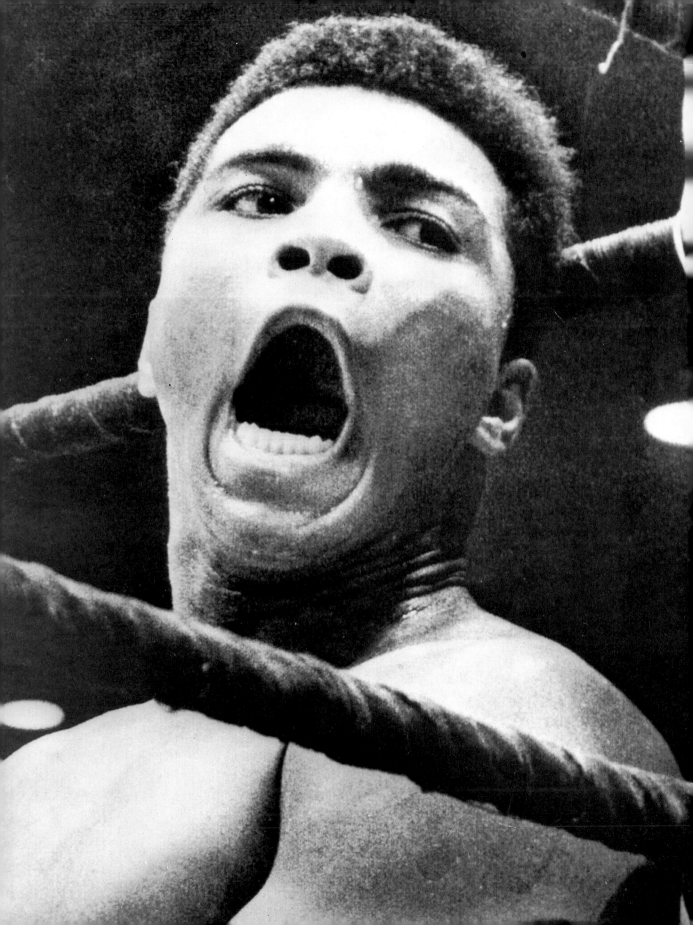

Martin Luther King changed American history by making the Constitution come good on its promises. Facing armed hatred with nothing but their bare hands, King and his followers showed a bravery which defied belief. J. Edgar Hoover bugged him in the attempt to discredit the Civil Rights movement by exposing him as a womanizer. He was, but so was President Kennedy. It was President Johnson who honoured King with the legislation that finally enforced voter registration in the South.

'I am the greatest!' shouted Cassius Clay, and he spoke nothing but the truth. In his first great fights for the World Professional Heavyweight Championship he wore the opposition out by dancing away from them and then helped them downwards to obscurity with an almost friendly flurry of not very heavy blows. Not falling for the idea that racism in America was over just because a few young, gifted blacks had made it out of the ghetto, he embraced another political no-no in the form of Islam, but at least he got a new name, Muhammad Ali. As a talk show guest he decked one host after another. His fame caught up with him when he fell prey to the notion that he could defy the laws of economics. In debt and trying for a comeback once too often, he sustained damage to the unique brain that had helped to make him the most famous boxer of the century. On his next talk show the guest was no brighter than the host.

the sky like the ash of an exploding volcano. From all over the world the cry converged on the USA: 'Physician, heal thyself.' But who would *be* the physician?

It wasn't going to be Lyndon Baines Johnson. The dead President Kennedy's successor had a hard act to follow. LBJ wasn't glamorous. He was an old-style, wheeler-dealer, porkbarrel pol whose *modus operandi* was a shoulder-squeeze in a smoke-filled room reverberating to the ring of the spittoon. When he spoke in public he sounded like a joke. The facts said that he was a masterly Mr Fix who could back up his cornpone rhetoric about the Great Society with a track record of liberal legislation better than Kennedy's. But JFK had turned the Presidency into a beauty contest and LBJ lost it. Vietnam was too big to fix. The young who ruled the world were singing, 'Hey hey hey, LBJ, how many kids did you kill today?' He had achieved anti-fame. Time to quit. He announced that he would not seek re-election for another term.

Robert Kennedy offered himself for the job. He had built his career as a committee-room inquisitor not much more scrupulous than Nixon, and he almost totally lacked his elder brother's charm. But RFK knew that JFK's fame, intensified by early death, would work for him too. It worked for the whole family. When JFK's widow Jackie formed an alliance with Aristotle Onassis, her behaviour was judged on the basis that she was a Kennedy. If she had still been Jacqueline Bouvier no one would have batted an eye. As things were, for JFK's widow to embrace a shipowner in elevator shoes was regarded as a step down in every sense. There were few to say that she had little choice except to seek protection: she was too famous to be out alone. To carry the Kennedy name was to wear a target.

The only refuge was in hiding and Bobby had left that far behind, on his way to the Presidency in a ball of light. He got as far as a kitchen in Los Angeles, where Sirhan Sirhan claimed his share of the dubious fame earned by Lee Harvey Oswald. Once again the world's TV screens filled with the slow, sad spectacle of a Kennedy funeral. Whether Bobby Kennedy, had he lived to be elected, would have achieved the seemingly eternal lustre of his elder brother remained an open question. But there was no doubt that he could never have started on the same course if JFK's mantle had not been there for him to borrow. Fame, like the funeral, had become part of the Kennedy inheritance.

Richard Nixon resented that and he had a point. The American Dream said that anyone could hope to be President. It didn't say that a single family could tie the job up. Nixon was elected fair and square by the people to whom he gave a voice – the silent majority. For the vocal minority, which included all the youth-oriented media, he was the villain. The spotlight which had given JFK a halo but had helped to melt LBJ was shining just as hot for Nixon. Every word he said, every little gesture, was marked for style and usually marked low.

Nixon's earlier fame as the candidate who wasn't charming like JFK was now redoubled. He was the President who wasn't charming like JFK and had the gall to be alive instead. The new habit of regarding the President as the personification of his country worked against him. People who saw America as the cruel enemy of freedom in Vietnam thought that Nixon was the walking, talking, deviously smiling personification of a system whose true nature had finally been revealed. At best Nixon was grudgingly admired for his tactical agility. But there was little love even from his supporters; and from his opponents, who seemed to include all the young people in the Western world, there was outright hatred from the first day he took office.

In the Eastern world, in that same famous year of 1968, the Russian leader Leonid Brezhnev became as famous as he was ever going to get when he personally ordered that Czechoslovakia's bid for freedom should be flattened with tanks. The Western world's young people were ready to concede that the Soviet Union might be almost as bad as America, but they found Brezhnev harder to hate than Nixon. Lenin had been injected with formaldehyde after death. Brezhnev had apparently received the same treatment while still alive. In his homeland he organized a personality cult for himself which ensured that his face was up on every building like a poster for the Russian version of *Planet of the Apes*. But with so little personality to make a cult of, his fame had no focus. Even as a villain, Brezhnev was a non-starter: tough on the Czechs, maybe, but strictly a zombie.

Even if you thought the main reason why American culture was so open to attack was because everybody lived in it and knew all the details, there was no denying that Charles Manson was convincing evidence of a society in the process of civic breakdown. Manson was a would-be rock star. After auditioning unsuccessfully for the Monkees he set himself up as a youth culture guru and continued the quest for fame. On the way he and his followers killed Roman Polanski's wife, Sharon Tate, and several other innocent people.

Is it Neil Armstrong? No, it's Buzz Aldrin. Armstrong is the reflection in his visor. But people think this is a photograph of Armstrong and it doesn't make much difference. The American astronauts were all the same man with slightly different wives. It was one of the requirements for a long, detailed, precise and fundamentally tedious journey – low volatility.

As an artist, Andy Warhol would have suffered from not enough talent if he had not chanced into a context where too much talent was a drawback – New York at the moment when fashion became an ideology. With no inner artistic imperative to follow, he was free to adapt his output – paintings, prints, films, parties, aphorisms – to what he guessed the media would next find outrageous enough to hail as a breakthrough. It was a value-free outlook, tested almost to destruction when one of his own bit players shot him.

The killings were unusually repellent in their satanic cruelty, but almost equally repellent was the fact that Manson achieved the fame he longed for. Media coverage was total and he revelled in it. His girl assistant, Squeaky Fromme, really seemed to think that she had made something of herself. The Manson family were tried and convicted but gaol walls were not enough to keep the media out. Anything Manson said showed up in print. Manson had star quality.

Twentieth-century fame had always been a value-free commodity. The notion that its freedom from value might be a value in itself – that famous people inhabited a world worth more than ours even when they were worthless – was promoted by the New York artist and style guru Andy Warhol. He first won fame for pop paintings that looked as if anyone could have painted them. He won further fame for making movies that looked as if anyone could have made them. His fame was doubled when he signed his name to silk-screen posters of other famous people, increasing their posthumous fame while causing some experts in pharmacology to observe that he looked as if he had already achieved posthumous fame while he was still alive.

His fame was redoubled when one of his followers shot him. Unlike Martin Luther King or the Kennedy brothers, Warhol survived – some said because he had been so near death from drugs already that his body didn't notice the bullet. But what made Warhol lastingly famous was his announcement that in the future everyone would be famous for fifteen minutes. Whether or not it was accurate as a prediction, it certainly matched the temper of the times. Look at Andy. If anyone ever looked like nobody, it was Andy Warhol: and think how far he had gone.

And think how far Neil Armstrong was going. He was an American astronaut and he was going to the moon. The same could have been said of Buzz Aldrin and Michael Collins, the other crew members on the mission. Or it could have been any other name from the whole team of astronauts on the project. Armstrong was chosen to be the man who would actually step on to the moon first for two main reasons. The first reason was not necessarily for publication: he was the dispensable one. If anything went wrong, the others knew how to get the mission home without him. The second reason was the one fed to the media. Armstrong was held to possess the right qualities of utter dependability and dedication.

But all the other astronauts possessed those qualities too. They were all long on virtue and short on individual characteristics. As personalities they barely registered. A better candidate would have been Captain James T. Kirk of the Starship *Enterprise*. In real life he was the actor William Shatner, but for the television audience across America, across the world, and perhaps one day across the galaxy, Kirk was the only way an astronaut should be. He said great things: 'Beam me up, Scotty.' He did great deeds. He wore, as space-time went by, an increasingly famous wig.

Unfortunately Kirk was fiction and NASA was stuck with the facts. Armstrong did his best to rise to the historic moment. He prepared a line which he would say when he stepped on to the moon's surface: 'That's one small step for a man, one giant leap for mankind.' He blew the line. He said 'man' instead of 'a man'. Since 'man' and 'mankind' are the same thing, what he said was strictly meaningless. But it didn't really matter what he said. He didn't need eloquence. He didn't even need a personality. Neil Armstrong was the century's most illustrious example of the Fonck Factor, the law by which, if the French aviator René Fonck had beaten Charles Lindbergh across the Atlantic, *he* would have got the glory. Armstrong could have been someone else and the result would have been the same. He was world-famous without ever having emerged from obscurity.

The man with the personality was there to welcome the moon hero back from space and bathe in the reflected glory. JFK had set the project up and Nixon reaped the reward. Nixon was not as flagrant as LBJ, who had been so keen to be associated with orbiting astronauts that he would have caught them in his outstretched arms when they returned to Earth if he had been allowed to. Nixon knew how to play the scene. Cynics said that Tricky Dick was up to his usual games. But maybe the bad guy was the right guy for the job. If America could conquer space, it might, with Nixon at the controls, work the other trick, and bring all those other boys back home from the mud. Suddenly Nixon was looking like the man. With no good name to lose, everything he could bring off was a plus. More scrutinized than any President in history, thrown on to a bonfire of bad publicity, he had risen from the blaze like a Phoenix. The most famous man in the world, he had nothing left to fear – unless of course, not that it was likely, he did something stupid.

CHAPTER SEVEN

TOWERING EARTHQUAKE
1969–1981

In the quarter of the twentieth century since World War II, America's position as the world's dominant cultural power had grown beyond challenge. Could the Russians produce an Elvis Presley? Where was the Chinese Frank Sinatra? No, America decided who became world-famous and the most famous American, the President, was the focus of the whole world's attention – even when he played with a yo-yo, was seen in public with Spiro Agnew, or turned out to have two close friends called Bebe Rebozo and Bob Ablanalp.

President Nixon was short of style. Still painfully aware that Jack Kennedy's charm was not among his own attributes, Nixon admitted that he lacked charisma. He could have been less nervous about making the admission. Nixon's abilities were real. Kennedy had been famous for inviting Pablo Casals to play in the White House. But when Nixon invited Duke Ellington, Nixon could do what Kennedy had never actually been able to – he could play the piano. So Nixon performed one of his own compositions on television. By nature he would never be entirely comfortable with the medium, but he looked less uncomfortable all the time. A lot of people out there were as awkward as he was. *They* weren't glamour-pusses either. Young long-hairs who smoked illicit substances mightn't like him, but most people with a stake in the set-up thought Nixon was at least competent. His notorious tricksiness turned into fame for being hard to fool. Nixon wouldn't do anything stupid out of misplaced romanticism. The heavy had become the leading man.

The leading man took on a sidekick, Henry Kissinger. Kissinger was Nixon's roving troubleshooter on foreign policy. He had a foreign accent to match. Kissinger never learned to speak like an American because he never listened. He was a bright man who always knew best. But he had one weakness. He simply loved being famous, because it made tall women love him. Here was the century's clearest proof that fame really must be an aphrodisiac. With Kissinger to advise him, Nixon turned the world stage from a metaphor into a fact. He actually went to China instead of just sending messages. By being there, he identified

As Nixon's right-hand man in foreign policy, Henry Kissinger got to press the flesh of every world leader up to and including Leonid Brezhnev, the Soviet leader who looked like a bit player from *Planet of the Apes*. Like Brezhnev, Kissinger hadn't actually been elected by anybody, but his position helped make him so famous as a geo-political superbrain that his future as a consultant on weighty matters was secure for life.

American worldwide influence with himself. Go anywhere, do anything. He went to Moscow and did the same thing again. Nixon was making it look like America's world. Somewhere back there behind the Kremlin, Brezhnev had a secret collection of American cars. Nixon wasn't collecting Russian ones. He was there to prove that he had the moral edge, the historic stature.

Vietnam looked like the only thing Nixon couldn't fix with a personal appearance. For young people at home and abroad, the war was his fault. Some of the more reprehensible aspects of it undoubtedly were. Nixon and Kissinger conspired to bomb Cambodia without Congress finding out. It was illegal, and when the news leaked many Americans of good heart began to despair of their system of government. Jane Fonda was a famous young film star from a family of film stars. She first came to prominence as a back-combed mindless love object in *Barbarella*. But the film's director, Roger Vadim, helped introduce her to the world of ideas. One of the ideas was that a female film star should be something more than a sex symbol. Reborn as a politically aware person, Fonda was admired by all for trying to make intelligent films. She got a more mixed reception when she tried to make political points. First she came out against the Vietnam War. Then she risked her career by going to Hanoi in protest at her own country's aggressive policy towards innocent freedom fighters. The innocent freedom fighters were delighted when she agreed to pose on an anti-aircraft gun otherwise employed to shoot down American bombers. Staking her fame on a point of principle made Fonda more famous than ever, but she came home with no guarantee that she would ever be allowed to star in films again.

If Nixon had had his way, she wouldn't have. Behind the scenes, he set the tax authorities to harass famous enemies while upfront he was gladhanding his famous friends, who gladhanded him right back. One of them was Frank Sinatra, who had switched allegiances after the Kennedys, worried about the bad publicity attached to his alleged Mafia connections, shut him out. Since it was not unknown that JFK had shared a mistress with a mobster, Sinatra had a right to feel hard done by. And the hard done by were Nixon's constituency.

It looked as if Nixon and his buddy Henry could handle anything. The silent majority knew that, if the only way out of Vietnam was to do a deal, then Dick and Henry would be the ones to do it. Nixon had proved that he was the one with the staying power. When the going gets tough the tough get going. It was his favourite saying. *Patton* was his favourite movie. But all the media attention that made it look as if Mister Fix wasn't so bad after all couldn't be turned off when it transpired that a private commando group financed by CREEP, the committee to re-elect him, had broken into the Watergate complex in Washington with the intention of bugging Democratic Party headquarters. Weatherbeaten political observers who knew that Presidents had always done unsavoury things were stunned only because Nixon hadn't needed to do something so risky. He was going to win anyway. But for young idealists everywhere Watergate was heaven sent. The villain who had been threatening to turn into a tough-guy hero was back to being a villain again, and this time he was double-dyed.

The villain fought a long and bitter rearguard action. If he had been a snowman he might have melted quickly. But he was up there on the world's television screens for ages, denying the undeniable. He had kept tapes of everything he said in the Oval Office. When the Senate Committee forced him to hand them over, he coughed up an edited version from which the crucial conversations were magically missing. Enough bad language was left in for the media to hang him all over again, but Nixon didn't have to curse to stand self-condemned. When he started admitting some of what he had previously been denying, coming clean sounded as furtive as the cover-up.

Nixon had disgraced himself and desecrated the Presidency. He brought fame itself into doubt. A world of sceptics had been created, who from now on would always wonder about the real story behind the aura. The sneaking suspicion that Mother Teresa might really be after a recording contract started with Nixon. Vietnam was just a lost war. When Nixon left the White House, it was a lost world. No American public official above the rank of dog-catcher would ever be fully trusted again.

After Watergate, the American public was ready for a heartwarming movie that showed healthy family values at work, even if the family were gangsters. *The Godfather* was made before the crisis burst but could now be seen in its full significance. All of Marlon Brando's old fame plus a slice more returned when he played Don Corleone. Brando as the all-seeing, all-wise head mobster was a fantasy that the worldwide audience wished was real: an

President Nixon (above left) at the moment of his resignation from office. Twenty years later he was still trying for a comeback on the world scene, believing, with some justification, that he had unequalled experience. Until Watergate the American public agreed, despite his well-attested record of calumniating his political opponents. The voters wanted a realist. The Watergate caper finished him not just because it was an unconstitutional manoeuvre but because he hadn't needed to do it, it didn't work, and the cover-up didn't work either.

The fame of Marlon Brando (above right) came back with all its old force in *The Godfather*, made while Nixon was still President. Brando stuffed his cheeks with cotton wool and played a Presidential head gangster with few scruples but much wisdom. After Nixon's fall Don Corleone started looking like the kind of President America needed. Later on, Brando's fame acquired a horrible, perhaps inevitable new twist when his son shot his daughter's boyfriend and Brando had to leave his Pacific island fortress to do what he was temperamentally least equipped for – throw himself on the mercy of the media.

In her first incarnation, Jane Fonda was the bimbo in *Barbarella*. Reborn as a politically aware person, she appeared at one point to be under the impression that she had personally brought the Vietnam War to an end. As a businesswoman she launched an aerobics craze that affected the musculature and vocabulary of a whole generation of American women. As a superstar she could set up any movie up to and including that ultimate test of bankability, the story about the Mexican rebellion. Through every transmogrification she remained unfailingly nice and enviably talented.

American President who knew what was going on and did not screw up. Off screen, however, Brando was not the man in charge, he was just a famous actor, and he was more trouble than he was worth. Nobody much minded the way he used his fame to make a fuss about the American Indians. After all, it wasn't as bad as Jane Fonda making a fuss about the North Vietnamese. But Brando didn't just use his power to fight the government. He used it to fight Hollywood. It had got to the point where nobody would bankroll a movie with him as the star. There was a nagging fear that he might eat the budget.

As Brando's girth grew huge, he left a vacuum into which a new generation of screen stars was eager to expand. They didn't let the system run them. They ran it. The press called them superstars. In the trade they were called gorillas. The most engaging gorilla was Jack Nicholson. After a long apprenticeship in obscurity he had become famous in the late sixties in *Easy Rider*, playing the sceptical lawyer who was too smart for the system. In the seventies he played the same part on screen and off. Even in *One Flew Over the Cuckoo's Nest*, when he was supposed to be a madman, he was a sane madman. It was the system that was insane. The only hope was to live by your own rules. Nicholson did this off screen as well as on. He said and did what he felt like. He also ate what he felt like and did nothing about his thinning hair except sketch in a bit of extra darkness with eyebrow pencil. Nicholson's core audience was the original youth culture growing older along with him. He was their proof that a first generation *Rolling Stone* reader could make millions of dollars and not lose touch with his Grateful Dead albums.

Warren Beatty was another gorilla who made his own rules. On screen his appeal consisted mainly of an improbably handsome face and a touching conviction that if he spent a long time searching for a word it added up to drama. But off screen he built up a reputation rivalling Errol Flynn's for his prowess as a seducer. He did this mainly by spending a long time searching for a word while current, ex- and would-be girlfriends revealed all to the press. He also took a long time searching for the right films, which were hardly ever as successful as his publicity. No star talked less and no star was more talked about. It was uncannily good career management and it was all his idea. Warren was in business for himself.

Clint Eastwood was an industry by himself. Of all the gorillas, he did the most thorough job of starting his own branch of the film business and running it on corporate lines. Before Watergate he starred in a string of westerns playing a mysterious bounty hunter who said virtually nothing while the music did all the talking. After Watergate Eastwood continued with the westerns but shifted his main marketing emphasis to an alternative line of product featuring himself as a cop fighting a lone battle against crime, his own police department, and the strange reluctance of soft-bellied liberals to put the bad guys away for good. His co-star was the biggest gun not mounted on a battleship. Eastwood had Magnum Force – his fame. Hollywood was a den of thieves but he had it beaten. He set up his own movies, took his cut up front, owned a percentage of the gross, and employed all the people who would once have been employing him.

Robert De Niro had even more guns than Clint Eastwood. In *Taxi Driver* he was a one-man arsenal and as mad as a hatter. De Niro studied taxi driving and madness in order to play the role. When he had to play Jake La Motta, a boxer who got fat, De Niro put on fifty pounds, something not even Marlon Brando had done deliberately. De Niro changed himself so completely for each role that the public had trouble remembering what he looked like. But everyone knew his name. He was Hollywood's first choice of star for any role meant to portray the psychosis, squalor and generally irredeemable sleaze of life in America.

The most unlikely gorilla was Robert Redford because he was boyishly clean-cut and innocent in the old teen-movie manner. But now that almost every starring role was about a man alone against corruption and hypocrisy, not even Redford could get away with being a conventional hero on the side of the law. Reprising the sixties' hit *Butch Cassidy and the Sundance Kid*, the story of a couple of lovable outlaws, Redford and Paul Newman had a huge seventies' hit with *The Sting,* the story of a couple of lovable con-men. Redford was so famous that any movie he wanted to make got made. He and the other gorillas had the movie business tied up. It was pure power. In Redford's case power never looked more pure – his teeth were so *friendly* – but power was what it was: the power of fame.

The new famous film stars knew all the rules of being famous film stars, and the new famous TV stars knew all the rules of being famous TV stars. There had been a time when a star stuck in a TV series dreamed only of graduating into the movies, like Clint Eastwood and Steve McQueen. But now TV stardom had its own sky for a limit. Every film star except

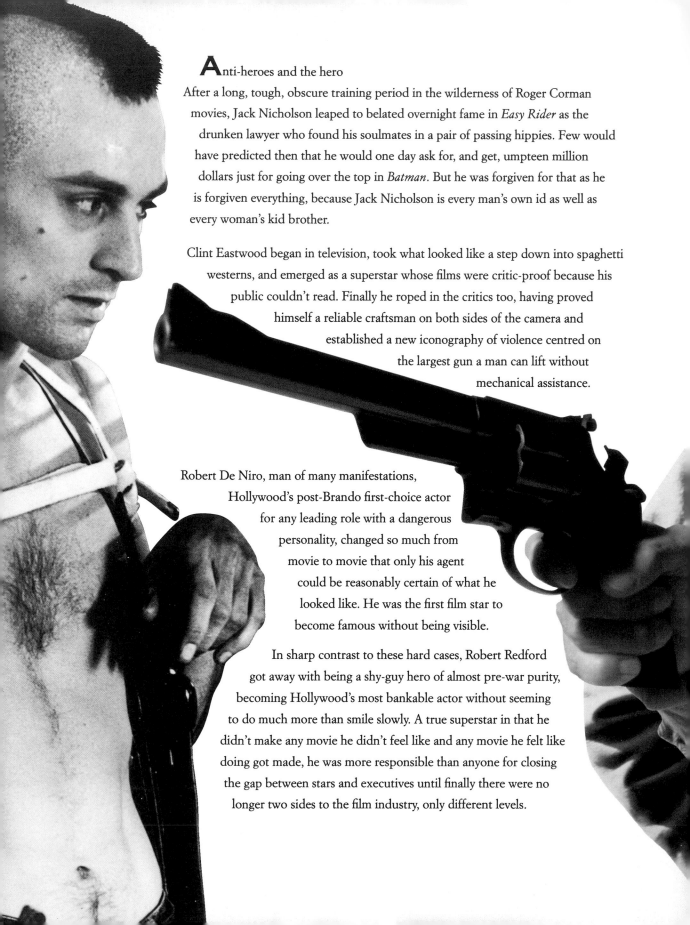

Anti-heroes and the hero

After a long, tough, obscure training period in the wilderness of Roger Corman movies, Jack Nicholson leaped to belated overnight fame in *Easy Rider* as the drunken lawyer who found his soulmates in a pair of passing hippies. Few would have predicted then that he would one day ask for, and get, umpteen million dollars just for going over the top in *Batman*. But he was forgiven for that as he is forgiven everything, because Jack Nicholson is every man's own id as well as every woman's kid brother.

Clint Eastwood began in television, took what looked like a step down into spaghetti westerns, and emerged as a superstar whose films were critic-proof because his public couldn't read. Finally he roped in the critics too, having proved himself a reliable craftsman on both sides of the camera and established a new iconography of violence centred on the largest gun a man can lift without mechanical assistance.

Robert De Niro, man of many manifestations, Hollywood's post-Brando first-choice actor for any leading role with a dangerous personality, changed so much from movie to movie that only his agent could be reasonably certain of what he looked like. He was the first film star to become famous without being visible.

In sharp contrast to these hard cases, Robert Redford got away with being a shy-guy hero of almost pre-war purity, becoming Hollywood's most bankable actor without seeming to do much more than smile slowly. A true superstar in that he didn't make any movie he didn't feel like and any movie he felt like doing got made, he was more responsible than anyone for closing the gap between stars and executives until finally there were no longer two sides to the film industry, only different levels.

Redford was playing criminals and psychos. The small screen was wide open for the maverick crimefighter. He worked outside the system, with the implication that the system could not be trusted to deliver justice. Starring in *Ironside*, Raymond Burr was a crippled President like FDR with the mind of Sherlock Holmes. He also had a dedicated team of assistants who called him 'Chief'. But essentially he was a law unto himself. The man of integrity within was unhampered by his injuries. The only downside of being Ironside was that the popular press called him Ironside far more often than they called him Raymond Burr.

William Conrad was Cannon, another maverick crimefighter with a physical problem. Cannon's handicap was an acute food dependency. But the man of integrity within was untouched. William Conrad had been a feature-list actor in movies. In TV he was an international star. Once again, the only drawback was that the popular press hardly ever remembered the name William Conrad. Yet people all over the world remembered the name Cannon. The expression 'William Conrad is Cannon' meant what it said.

Peter Falk was Columbo, yet another maverick crimefighter for a country which had come to believe that only a maverick crimefighter could get results. The man of integrity within was untouched by his dirty raincoat. Like all the other maverick crimefighters, Columbo could be easily exported to other countries. The initial costs were covered in the huge American domestic market, so the sell-on cost for export was low. But since the canny Falk had staved off over-exposure by restricting the supply of product to six episodes a year, the Bulgarian public panicked, thinking they were being deprived of Columbo by state censorship. Falk broadcast to Bulgaria to reassure that country's desperate population that he would be back – or rather that Columbo would.

The most normal-looking of the maverick crimefighters was James Garner in *The Rockford Files*. His movie career had been interesting but chancy. As Rockford he was working all the time, although he didn't know that the production company had an accounting system which would result in his share of the net profit disappearing into production expenses even though the gross profit was astronomical. Garner's trusting nature fitted the character. Rockford was an honest poor man fighting the corrupt rich. His house was a trailer and he was the man of integrity within. Garner was Rockford, Rockford took Garner over, and Garner was never quite as famous as Rockford again.

The most maverick of the maverick crimefighters was Kojak, played by Telly Savalas. Savalas was a prominent name in the feature list of some big movies. But Kojak was a big television name all over the world. Kojak's catchphrase was translated into most of the languages on Earth: 'Who loves ya, baby?' American television software was taking over the global market like Japanese television hardware, and the star got world-famous along with it. But international television fame was a kind of half fame, like the moon. The dark side was the actor's name. The bright side was the character's name. Kojak. Anyone could say that.

International television had become a highly efficient way of making almost anything world-famous, but an act that appealed to the whole family got most famous. And if a whole family *was* the act, then the result was the Osmonds, the most effective weapon of cultural aggression America had developed since flavoured chewing gum. The Osmonds were a multiple independently targeted re-entry vehicle which went off in the world's households and injected every member of the family with a lethal dose of neat sugar. There was someone in the Osmond family for everyone to love. Teenage girls loved Donny, whose teeth were so dazzling, and so numerous, that it was difficult to count them. It was an open question who loved little Jimmy. The appeal of the nubile Marie was more easily explained, although there was a Julie Andrews-type wholesomeness factor which tended to set limits to illicit lust.

As they died off, older members of the family could presumably always be replaced from an apparently infinite supply of younger ones. So there seemed, on the face of it, no reason why the Osmonds should not go on for ever. The Osmonds themselves were less disposed to put faith in the extended life of a fad. As good Mormons they turned over a tenth of their enormous earnings to the tabernacle, invested the rest, lived clean and counted their blessings.

For older and spiritually less focussed entertainers in search of a version of eternal life that had twenty-four-hour room service, Las Vegas turned into a place where they could grow old gracelessly. It was a kind of elephants' graveyard where they sold their own ivory before crashing to their knees for the last time. F. Scott Fitzgerald had once famously said that there were no second acts in American lives. Elvis Presley proved that his life did have

As the whole world became a single outlet for television series manufactured in the United States, American TV actors were no longer less famous than movie actors. They were more famous but not under their own names. The name of the character got the recognition and the man with his name on the payslip took a back seat. Kojak was more famous than Telly Savalas; Columbo than Peter Falk; Cannon than William Conrad; Ironside than Raymond Burr. Even more famous than any of the maverick crimefighters was the charming monster from *Dallas*, J. R. Ewing – who was in turn far more famous than Larry Hagman.

a second act, and it was a farce. He performed as a parody of himself, kept in motion by the memory of his old mannerisms and chemical assistance administered by various means. Projected from Las Vegas to the waiting world, his image was of an historical figure raking through his own filing cabinets in search of raw material. There was nothing new. His only triumph was still to be there. He was a man in his prime reminiscing like an old-age pensioner, practising to be a memory.

Liberace's later phase was undignified too, but in a less degrading way because he had never been dignified in the first place. Glitz had always been his thing and in Vegas he took it to the point of apocalypse. To the millions of blue-rinsed mothers who had always loved him he was beginning to look like one of them. To observers out there in the civilized world, the American celebrity register had begun to look like a graveyard of the living dead. It was as if bodysnatchers from space had turned famous people into zombies programmed to be themselves forever, with an endless supply of wigs and a permanently renewable annual appointment with the plastic surgeon.

Frank Sinatra started an alarming cycle of saying goodbye and then returning. His first return happened before anyone realized he had been away. It was announced with the slogan: 'Ol' Blue-Eyes is back'. No one had ever called him Ol' Blue-Eyes. The slogan was thought up by an ad man. The way the press swallowed it for worldwide regurgitation tipped off everyone in the celebrity business that there was now so much media attention available that no story could fail. At Sinatra's forty-years-in-showbiz concert all his famous acquaintances turned out to compete with each other on worldwide television in proving how well they knew him. His friend Sammy Davis Junior was only the runner-up. The winner was Orson Welles, whose gustatory habits had given the bodysnatchers a lot to work on. Welles rose hugely to the challenge of extolling Sinatra's virtues, calling him a pirate and a pussycat. 'And ultimately and forever,' growled Welles fondly, 'he is undefeated.' He made Sinatra sound like London in the Blitz.

Welles still dreamed of making movies and from time to time actually did so, but what he mainly did was make commercials. Trading on his fame as a genius, he recommended upmarket goods for financial reward. A brand of booze heard itself being plugged as 'probably' the finest in existence. It paid the hotel bills. Finally he was not even a body, just a voice. Welles the voice-over graced enough commercials to keep him alive. When he died, mimics continued the work, convincing the listener that Welles was in some sense still active, searching out 'probably' peerless products to satisfy his discriminating taste. The fame he had earned as a boy genius had lasted him a lifetime, and beyond.

Fame had become a branch of eternity where what you did might be forgotten but your name would live always, because even if you buried yourself the media would dig you up again. Las Vegas was the last refuge of the billionaire eccentric Howard Hughes. In a guarded hotel suite, doing nothing except grow his hair and fingernails until they threatened to fill the bedroom, he sought oblivion. His punishment was to be remembered. The media remembered his pre-war record-breaking feats with aeroplanes. They remembered his record-breaking feats with women. They remembered the huge flying boat he designed that never flew more than a hundred yards. They remembered the bra he designed to lift Jane Russell's bosom into the firing position. They remembered everything about him, but still couldn't figure out that the real reason why he had run and hid was because he remembered them.

Hughes, as rich as any monarch and with more freedom of action, had chosen not to live with his fame. It raised the question of whether those other famous old people would go on riding the bandwagon if they knew how to get off. Few of them had enough power to choose, and certainly not the film stars. Prisoners of an expensive way of life, most of them kept working even when they were no longer in a position to choose their work. The disaster movie was a typical post-Watergate exercise in absolute cynicism. Its appeal depended on a plentiful supply of famous names to get killed off by the disaster. In *Earthquake*, Los Angeles was destroyed by a special effect. Ava Gardner, an ex-star, fell down a lift shaft. Charlton Heston lasted longer because he was still good for a few more leading roles, although only just. In *Towering Inferno*, a skyscraper was set alight by corrupt wiring installed by unscrupulous big business. Robert Wagner died in the flames. So did Richard Chamberlain. But Paul Newman and Steve McQueen both survived, because they were still bankable enough to insist. The disaster movie was the exact expression of what fame had become: the survival of the fittest. Management was everything.

Elizabeth Taylor and Richard Burton were a disaster movie all by themselves. They got married for the second time, seemingly for no other purpose except to stage a repeat performance of their well-established round of extravagance, ill-judged would-be artistic projects, well-publicized affection, better-publicized disaffection, disintegration and divorce. It was Towering Earthquake II. Together they were equal: two halves of a complete nightmare. But apart, Taylor knew how to live with her fame, because there was no real discrepancy between it and what she was capable of. She didn't get in its way. For Burton, nagged if not haunted by a sense that he might have done better things if his fame had not taken over his life, the prognosis was not so good.

A one-man disaster movie was President Gerald Ford, of whom ex-President Johnson cruelly said that he had played too much football without his helmet. The second famous Ford of the century was no relation to Henry and no comparison either. The press picked up on his physical clumsiness and ruled him out of contention for heroic status. America's new and unprecedented fear that it might no longer be in control of events was reflected in the behaviour of its heroes, who, even if they did well, seemed to be representing themselves rather than their country.

The swimmer Mark Spitz won more Olympic gold medals than Johnny Weissmuller. But his chief aim in life was to translate his fame as a sportsman into a career as a pop singer. As a pop singer he was a swimmer who breathed in at the wrong moment, and drowned. America had a world chess champion, Bobby Fischer. The whole world knew his name, but not because he was America's great chess player. It was because he was America's great maniac. The Russian champion Boris Spassky was sane by comparison, since he was merely inclined to suspect electronic surveillance by the CIA and walk in fear of poisoned yogurt. He was right to be paranoid about Fischer, who kicked him under the table. Fischer beat Spassky at chess, but the Soviets came out of the contest looking more like a world power. America was turning out screwballs.

The Soviets had a huge PR success with their pre-pubescent champion gymnast Olga Korbut. Little Olga could do everything Americans had ever done. She was as precocious as Shirley Temple, no bigger than Mickey Mouse, she flew through the air like Superman and she could dance to pop music. The Russians were turning out prodigies. They turned out Solzhenitsyn altogether. Expelled by the KGB, he carried the message of his great book

In Las Vegas, Liberace found the context he had been looking for since birth – a showcase with such a tolerance for kitsch that he could go nova. The problem of how to be outrageous for an audience with no taste was finally solved.

On the night when Orson Welles received the Life Achievement Award from the American Film Institute, Frank Sinatra took the rare opportunity to embrace a legend bigger than his. Welles's lifetime achievement in film was a tenth of what he might have achieved, but then he would have had to be a different, less famous man.

The Gulag Archipelago to an astonished world. The book was an exposé of the Soviet Union's long-standing reign of terror against its own people and the world should not have been astonished. But Stalin's fame died hard and Lenin's remained unscathed. Solzhenitsyn's other message, the one about the West's shameful weakness in the face of the totalitarian threat, got a bigger response. Solzhenitsyn had heroic stature. He was telling the free world that it didn't.

Out of the newly discovered Third World came the kind of hero America was no longer supplying. Honest, modest, good-looking, supernaturally skilful, the Brazilian footballer Pelé personified soccer for all the countries in the world that played the game. That meant practically every country except America, and even America got the point about Pelé. Despite the unexciting results of his one-man match against President Ford, for a while soccer looked like becoming a boom sport there, just because Pelé was playing it.

Even more unknown than the Third World, Sweden produced Bjorn Borg. Sweden had been heard of because Greta Garbo and Ingrid Bergman had both left it. Some intellectuals had heard of it because the film director Ingmar Bergman had stayed there. But Borg dominated an international sport as his country's national idol. With ice-water for blood he came out of the North to carve his way through a corrupt civilization. The American champions played to the gallery. Borg just played, and won. Wise voices said what a relief it was to watch a young man hit the top and stay there without being distracted by fame or the lure of easy money. You couldn't imagine Borg turning himself into a T-shirt. The idea that the austere, herring-fed champion might have a future in fancy goods never crossed anyone's mind.

Tennis was the right-shaped sport for television, so the whole world could tune in to what was essentially a display of character. The American woman champion Billie Jean King occasionally shouted at herself, but never at anyone else. She had discipline. Chris Evert never shouted even at herself. She was so disciplined she was practically Borg-like. The American male champion Jimmy Connors, on the other hand, behaved badly when things went against him, and the supreme American male champion John McEnroe behaved badly all the time. Tennis players became measures of character in every household. Children were told: Don't be like McEnroe. Be like Borg.

The Mr Nice Guy of the tennis boom, succeeding Australia's Rod Laver and John Newcombe in the role of Wimbledon's modest multiple champ, Sweden's Bjorn Borg (left), with his impeccable behaviour and rare ability to tell the press absolutely nothing, was hailed by his admirers as some kind of philosopher. Only later was it revealed that fame had done things to his head which no head-band, no matter how tightly adjusted, could control, and that he was just another poor dumb-cluck who wanted to get married in a pink tracksuit.

The only tennis player famous enough to be watched by people who weren't interested in tennis, John McEnroe (right) broke the unwritten contract by which someone blessed with a supreme gift is supposed to acknowledge that it belongs to the world. He behaved as if it belonged to him, throwing tantrums which challenged the officials either to deprive the tournament of half its interest by disqualifying him, or else to bring their rule book into disrepute by letting him get away with it. They let him get away with it.

Another Swedish world hit was Abba, a pop quartet who turned themselves into Sweden's second biggest export money-earner after Volvo. Four people with unpronounceable names were doing what the Beatles once did: churn out hit singles you couldn't help singing along with while you danced to them, and vice versa. Abba didn't sing their songs in Swedish, but on the other hand their English didn't sound American. It was a new style of Euro-English, the first sign that the Common Market might have a say in the world's common culture. The four faces of Abba were famous everywhere in the world, even though the number of people who could pronounce the name Agnetha Faltskog never increased beyond her immediate family.

Even more outlandish than Sweden was Hong Kong, whence arose the significant figure of Bruce Lee, kick-boxing star of the kung-fu movies that swept first the cinemas of the Far East, then the Chinatowns of all the world's big cities, and finally everywhere that powerless people dreamed of paralysing their oppressors with a sudden outburst of uncanny martial arts. Before Bruce Lee, the typical kung-fu movie had been just an endless succession of fight sequences featuring the hero kicking the heavies while the soundtrack matched even the most fleeting blow with the sound of a sledgehammer hitting a crate of eggs. Bruce revolutionized the form. With him as the star, the typical kung-fu movie remained exactly the same but with an added ingredient: Bruce's spiritual sensitivity. As the first truly idealistic kung-fu star, he gave the audience something Charles Bronson couldn't, even with the most thoughtfully arranged wig. Bruce Lee was a philosopher. He fought crime out of his unshakeable conviction that a pure life was possible. In a world that had come to be ruled by fear, he dared to dream.

Even more outlandish than Hong Kong, in fact unearthly, was outer space, whence came the sexually ambiguous pop superstar David Bowie. In his earthly existence he had been an Englishman whose real name was David Jones, but after a tour of the outer galaxies he had returned to this planet as some kind of extraterrestrial transsexual. Parents in the sixties had been worried that their children would have their minds bent by drugs. Parents in the seventies, some of whom had been the children of the sixties, were worried that *their* children would have their genders bent by Bowie. Though bisexuality was just sex twice and nothing could be safer than sex, fear was hard to quell. It was in the air.

Fastest fist in the East. Born in San Francisco, Bruce Lee rose in a flurry of flying feet to be the spring-heeled front-runner of martial arts movies made in Hong Kong. The Bruce Lee kung fu spectaculars captured a world market to make him the planet's most recognizable face after Muhammad Ali. Kung fu film buffs write learned articles about the supposedly balletic grace of Bruce Lee's fight sequences and the potency of the mind behind his fiercely concentrated frown. A more likely explanation of his cult status was that he provided fantasies of bare-handed omnipotence for people so poor they couldn't even dream of owning a gun.

A nightmare from West Germany that scared the world, the pampered and
lethal Andreas Baader and Ulrike Meinhof were terrorists in armed rebellion against
something called the Consumer Society. Since everyone who was not also in armed rebellion
against this entity was *ipso facto* an apologist for it, the inspired couple felt justified in killing
anybody at all. After they were captured, Meinhof added herself to the total. Baader
thought for a while before doing the same. Their name lived on as one person who
never actually existed, Baader-Meinhof.

The first terrorists to make it as media stars were the Germans Andreas Baader and Ulrike Meinhof. They killed innocent people deemed by them to be guilty of compliance with the ruthless capitalist system. They were famously hard to catch. After they *did* get caught they had no one left to kill except themselves. Ulrike was the one who did it first. She got famous all over again. Terror was a path to glory.

In America Patty Hearst was known only as the granddaughter of William Randolph Hearst, the man whose mass circulation newspapers had given twentieth-century fame its initial boost. Kidnapped by a tiny group of home-grown terrorists calling themselves the Symbionese Liberation Army, she showed up alongside them pulling a bank raid. Some said she had been brainwashed. Others said that she had simply found running around with guns and getting famous for it more fun than being anonymously rich. Few said, but all felt, that the veneer of civilization must be awfully thin if a few head-cases could stage their own revolution and grab world headlines.

In Uganda, Idi Amin had been just a sergeant when the British were still running the country. Now he was the man in charge and running the country into the ground, killing thousands while doing so. He was a head-hunter, but the world couldn't see that, even though some of the heads were in his refrigerator. What the world saw was a brilliantly successful stand-up comedian. Idi presented himself as a political genius equipped to solve the world's problems. When Britain went on a three-day week Idi proclaimed a Save Britain campaign, in his new capacity as King of Scotland. When terrorists hijacked a plane full of Israelis and landed in Entebbe, Amin detained the hostages to please his allies among the Arab nations. Israel raided Entebbe to get their people out, and Idi was famous all over again. He was never out of the headlines. When the Entebbe movies came out, his name was on the posters. The civilized world was uneasily aware that there wasn't a lot it could do except wait for his embarrassed neighbours to chase him away. He ended up in the Sands Hotel, Jeddah, giving interviews about his readiness to return to his grieving country. It was another stand-up routine. The Sands, Jeddah, was Idi's Las Vegas.

Even in its own eyes, America was a wimp in a world gone wild. The feeling of power-lessness was powerfully embodied by Woody Allen. He was an anti-hero hero, devoid of strength, his only dominance over words, an intellectual who understood everything but couldn't change it – a Nebbish. In real life Woody Allen was a superstar in the strict sense, a pint-sized gorilla whose sure-fire art-house appeal earned him the power to set up his own movies on a unique contract which gave him complete control over every detail of their manufacture. He used Hollywood as a means of artistic expression and didn't let Hollywood use him for anything. Instead of attending the Oscar ceremony he stayed in New York playing jazz. He had a succession of movie star girlfriends, and when the affair failed he made a successful movie about it. For everyone in the business he was the model of how fame could be managed. For everyone outside the business, he was the most famous example of what America had become – nervous.

Dustin Hoffman became famous in the sixties in *The Graduate*, playing a nervous young man who suspected that life in America was stacked against him. In the seventies he became more famous still as an even more nervous, slightly less young man who *knew* that life in America was stacked against him. He was small, put-upon and worried, like Woody Allen minus the wise-cracks. In *Kramer v Kramer* he was given a very bad time by the new female superstar Meryl Streep.

Hoffman looked as if he would be given a very bad time by anyone. The only American who looked and sounded as if he was still on top of it all was Muhammad Ali. This was the period of his greatest fame. The worldwide satellite-linked television network meant that he could fight in exotic places like Zaire or Manila and be watched by everyone. If the fight itself proved dull, or even if he lost it, he still came out ahead because he was unbeatable in the pre- and post-fight interviews. Faster with his mouth than any other boxer even though his feet were slowing up, Ali transferred his highly polished technique as an interviewee to the talk show circuit, where he made it clear that he was representing himself, not his country. He was a world champion, not an American champion. Fame was a storm and he knew how to ride it. He could manage.

So could Barbra Streisand. She was a new kind of American world heavyweight champion. She was the first female gorilla. Get her and you had a movie. Hear her and you had an earache, some said. But they were shouting into a hurricane. Streisand was Hollywood's first Jewish Princess who didn't have to play it Christian. She was so powerful she could play it as she pleased. Her albums sold in millions. She could open any Broadway show she felt like. Her television specials reached the world. She didn't need Hollywood, and Hollywood had always been impressed by that. It handed her the moon. She set up her own blockbuster movies. She didn't have to care what she wore to the Oscar ceremonies, even if, shot from the back in her black transparent pants-suit, she looked as if she was mooning in mourning. She didn't have to care what her co-stars thought about her prima donna behaviour. Walter Matthau said he'd love to work with her again, perhaps in *Macbeth*. She even dared not to show up for Johnny Carson's *Tonight Show*. Johnny fumed, but Barbra forged on. Feminists were a rising force and they admired Streisand for being herself, for not trying to get her funny looks fixed, for putting all those fat male Hollywood moguls in their place. She could manage.

From the same England as the Beatles but from a younger youth culture came the Sex Pistols, their five-minute mission to be so repulsive that they would never be assimilated. They accomplished it triumphantly. Everyone heard of them and almost no one knew who they were. Two of them were called Johnny Rotten and Sid Vicious, but unless you were a sixteen-year-old fan with a bolt through your neck and an earring in your nose it was hard to tell which was which. Eventually Vicious solved the problem by checking into a New York hotel and killing himself. So the one left over had to be Rotten. He sank back into the obscurity from which he had never really emerged, leaving the world with a suggestive example of what fame could do if it was cleverly enough manipulated: operate without people.

The last throes of Elvis Presley were like another group breaking up, since he had grown so bloated in decline. Death came as a merciful release from long-term drug and hamburger abuse. It came as a shock but no surprise. It was revealed that at the very moment when President Nixon had been enlisting his aid in the war on drugs, Elvis had been so high that his knees trembled even when he wasn't singing. Now, with his corpulent presence finally out of the way, his image was free from interference and fit to be resurrected. His Southern mansion, Graceland, where the architectural traditions of Walt Disney, Hugh Hefner and Liberace all came together in one transcendentally tasteless apotheosis, was incorporated as a cash-generating shrine. The field was free for Elvis Presley look-alikes to emerge, who with the aid of plastic surgery at least looked more like his image than he had ended up doing.

The decay of the angel. Elvis Presley in his downhill phase, when the deadly combination of drugs and hamburgers had produced results over which no zip would close, stuffing even the most generously designed buckskin jumpsuit until its fringes stiffened like quills. Most of the Elvis lookalikes already looked more like him than he did. There was only one logical career move left to make.

His career was easier to manage without him. The man was gone and his fame lived on. When his manager, Colonel Tom Parker, said that Elvis's death didn't change a thing he was understating the case. Elvis was a bigger hit dead than alive. He made more money in the three years after his death than in the whole of his previous career. Crucified by his first fame, he came back on the third day, to be resurrected into his second, eternal fame, a shining spirit in the electronic universe.

President Carter moved on too, but his destination was oblivion. Thoughtful and decent as a man, as a celebrity he had made all the wrong moves. The Southern Boys behind Carter had no idea of how to manage his fame. When he went running they let him try to finish the course instead of just jogging along for fifty yards and holding a press conference. The result was another disaster movie, with Carter sobbing for air in the arms of his embarrassed Secret Service men. Giving an interview to *Playboy* was merely ill-advised. Telling the truth in the interview was a disaster. He had said that he had committed adultery in his heart. For the sake of a few votes from the kind of men who could commit adultery with a fold-out photograph, Carter had sacrificed millions of votes from plain folks who wanted a President they could count on to be less worried about the world than they were. Carter capped it in the decisive pre-election debate when he revealed that his consultant on the subject of thermonuclear war was his daughter Amy.

With a wimp in the White House, there was a dangerous tendency to admire the devil in Dallas. The soap opera of the same name was dominated by a womanizing, wheeler-dealing oil tycoon whose name became one of the most famous on Earth. J. R. Ewing was the character's name. The actor's name was Larry Hagman and he was never as famous as the role he played. A one-time film actor who had been through the mill and come out ground small, Hagman knew exactly what he was doing in *Dallas*. While other characters were written out when the actors died or vainly tried to launch film careers, Hagman built his whole career around J.R. For journalists who wanted to write about the actor, Hagman kept a collection of funny hats to provide an easy talking point. But Hagman knew that the real fame was J.R.'s. On talk shows the actor matched his manner to the character's wicked grin. Somewhere behind the man pretending to be the real man pretending to be the character, the *real* real man was protecting his private existence. Letting your image get famous for you was a way of keeping control. But the image was out of control. It had a life of its own. The bad guy was in command.

America was up against it. The good guys were wimps and the bad guys had all the glamour. A good guy was needed who had glamour too, someone who knew how to seem like a hero, someone who knew how to handle fame, or at least had some back-up from people who knew how to handle him. The management of fame had become its essence. And fame management was so much easier if the man who was famous didn't interfere, and never said 'Where's the rest of me?' except in jest.

CHAPTER EIGHT

THE MONSTER WALKS AMONGST US

1981–1992

I n eighty years, less than the time some people live, fame in the twentieth century had paralleled the history of radioactivity, which had started off as a glow in the night in Madame Curie's backyard laboratory, gone through an unfortunate phase when it destroyed the lives of every human being it could reach, and ended up so well understood that if you followed the handbook you could run a power station with it. The force of fame, in all its poisonous radiance, had been tamed into something almost friendly.

Or so it appeared. At first nothing could appear more friendly than Ronald Reagan unless it started shaking hands with the surrounding scenery. Reagan was America's way back to the future. The world's leading power had felt its power slipping. Reagan's mere appearance promised to put things back the way they used to be, when Jimmy Stewart and Gary Cooper went to Washington, when John Wayne was worth a whole Japanese regiment, when Henry Fonda was President. And Reagan wouldn't be thrown by all the media attention. Reagan was used to fame. Presenting an image had been his life. Reagan, or the men behind him, offered simplicity. Reagan looked, talked and walked like an old-time movie hero who whipped the heavies in the last reel and got the girl.

He *was* an old-time movie hero. Now that political campaigning had moved almost completely to television, it depended on sound bites – a few phrases recited parrot fashion. Reagan was good at that, because he had been doing it since the days when it was called dialogue. Decades had gone by, but Reagan's delivery, like the colour of his hair, was miraculously unaltered. If anything, he had increased his capacity to sound perfectly sincere while saying in a relaxed manner something that he had memorized only with difficulty.

Some said that there was nothing else in Reagan's head except scraps of dialogue from old movies and commercials. They might have been right, but they were missing the point. Reagan's Presidency might be mainly a performance, it might not add up to anything more than making people feel good, but if his opponents poured all their efforts into mocking

A photograph to make anyone with even mildly left-wing political sympathies recall Gore Vidal's phrase about the two Broadway stars who got married: the rocks in his head fit the holes in hers. Yet although neither Margaret Thatcher nor Ronald Reagan would ever have been elected if socialist ideology had not first collapsed, both of them had the essential political gift of attracting loyalty from people cleverer than they were. Finally leadership, in any democracy, is a matter of character – a fact few intellectuals find palatable.

him, they were calling the majority of the population suckers. And anyway, there was more to him, or more behind him, than that. Reagan's free market message might be a recipe for fraudsters to get rich quick. But the other message, the one about the strong state that looked after the helpless, had no heroes left to represent it, partly because not enough people believed it.

Even if Reagan was all fame and nothing else, for now that was enough. There was no man in America to match him. The only man to match him was in Britain, and she was a woman. Margaret Thatcher carried on with all the confidence of Winston Churchill minus the cigar, drumming up memories of a Britain with a seat at the top table. Promising her country that it could rebuild itself, she offered an example by rebuilding *her*self. At the start she had the hair, teeth and voice of a woman who looked her age. Following the advice of carefully chosen image experts, she soon had the hair, teeth and voice of someone much younger.

Focusing all the attention on herself, she forced the Opposition into the fatal mistake of making personal attacks on her. It was a mistake because it was too easy. By upstaged males in her own party she was called Attila the Hen and a lot of other things less kind. For the satirists she would have been a sitting duck if she hadn't moved so fast. But she absorbed scorn like sunlight and photosynthesized it into energy. No parody by others could match her supremely confident self-parody of vim, decisiveness and bustle. Rumours that Queen Elizabeth II looked forward to her weekly visit from Mrs Thatcher like a visit to the dentist gained weight during the war over the Falkland Islands, when Mrs Thatcher started sounding like Queen Elizabeth I. Mrs Thatcher was born for fame, and the only question was whether her own country was a big enough stage to contain her.

The question was answered when she formed a rapport with Ronald Reagan that was the biggest transatlantic romance since Clark Gable embraced Vivien Leigh. When Mrs Thatcher visited Reagan in America, he announced to the world that her espousal of his free market principles was the greatest honour he could have. When Reagan visited Britain, she voiced the same sentiments about him. But the world knew that their relationship went beyond the mutual admiration of two dedicated supply-side economists. Ronnie and Maggie were two stars together, bathing in each other's glow.

With the possible exception of being naive enough to believe that her telephone calls wouldn't be intercepted by some lurking retired bank-manager with a dish aerial, she did everything right. In a role she had never had a chance to rehearse for, she was a triumph. But if anything pushed Fleet Street's concern with royalty beyond obsession and into a frenzy, it was the mere existence of the Princess of Wales: model, cover-girl, dancer, nurse, silent film star and walking constitutional crisis.

Like Jack and Jackie Kennedy before them, and Douglas Fairbanks and Mary Pickford before *them*, the Prince and Princess of Wales were the world's most famous perfect couple. It wasn't true because it couldn't be true. There is no such thing as the perfect couple: there is only a reasonably conducted private life, which the royal pair were eventually unable to lead, all concept of privacy having been destroyed by publicity of an intrusiveness unheard of since Hanoverian times, and on a scale that only the techniques of modern fame could have made possible.

Sylvester Stallone acted the part of Reagan's favourite dream – restored pride in America. Stallone started playing the part before Reagan came to power, when he created the role of *Rocky*, the boxing has-been who refused to lie down, the bum who came back. With Reagan safely installed in the White House Rocky came back again, in *Rocky II* and *Rocky III*, not to mention *Rocky IV*, proving over and over that in Reagan's rediscovered America a man didn't need welfare or any of that sissy stuff, that if he could just keep wearing down his opponent's fist by hitting it with his face he could make it on his own. But Stallone wasn't just a boxer with restored pride. In *First Blood* he established a whole new persona as a Vietnam veteran with restored pride. Rambo came back again in *Rambo II*, *Rambo III*, not to mention *Rambo IV*, proving over and over that one man on his own could still stand up to the bad guys as long as he had the right gun, grenades, rocket-launcher and attack helicopter. The way Stallone told it, Vietnam and any other mild overseas embarrassments were really victories, because they gave America the chance to rediscover its true character as a country where an individual could come back from defeat and achieve anything.

Stallone the man was living proof that an American could become his dream. Not content with the body nature had given him, he replaced it with a new one combining all the most impressive styling features of a 1950s' Detroit car. He discovered within himself the ability to be a painter, and developed it as he had worked on his pecs and lats. A living, bulging embodiment of Reagan's philosophy, Stallone identified power with the individual will. He was a one-man movement, attracting mass adulation because he didn't seem to need it, comfortably ridiculous because he didn't care who laughed. He was a comic-book hero. But the comic was read by adults – the kind of adults who got excited by a heavy-calibre, belt-fed phallic symbol. They weren't just American. Stallone's audience covered the planet. He was the new Bruce Lee, living out the fantasies of the helpless with all the power of American technology sticking out of his trousers.

J. R. Ewing's reign as the King of *Dallas* reached its apotheosis under Reagan. Now that corrupt America was passé and straight-arrow America was back in business, it was time for J.R. to get his. The shooting of J.R. was announced in advance all over the world. It was fictional, but it made news like fact. Even Britain's staid BBC ran a teaser during the evening news. The line between fact and fiction had become blurred and it was fame that did the blurring. J.R. was no longer an actor, he was a real man. He was more than that, he was a Messiah. He rose from the dead and continued with the next series, like a President going into his next term. Casual violence had been domesticated into a cartoon. It would have been good if things could have stayed that way. But reality was still there, and in reality someone shot John Lennon.

The assassin was a fan who had asked Lennon to autograph his *Double Fantasy* album only a few hours before. Mark Chapman thought he *was* John Lennon, the real John Lennon, the one who had not sold out. Lennon, who had come to New York to escape the madness of the Beatles' fame, had walked right back into it and it was holding a gun. The Lennon killing threw a lasting scare into every famous entertainer in America. Sudden death from a criminal had been understood since Lindbergh. Sudden death from a fan meant that fame was a cage you could never get out of. The best you could do was turn it into an electrified fence.

The growing suspicion that American fandom could be fatal became a certainty when Ronald Reagan himself got shot. This time the perpetrator wasn't a fan of the victim. John Hinckley was a fan of the film star Jodie Foster and he did it to impress her. He doubled her fame by doing so, but she would willingly have had it halved again. She was Hinckley's victim as surely as Reagan was. Her recovery was long and slow, and involved a strict ban on discussing the subject in interviews. Reagan's recovery was more rapid, as if he had played this scene before. Getting shot had given him a good chance to reform America's gun laws, but he didn't try. Either he was in the pocket of the National Rifle Association, or else he was sustained by his faith that if the good guy gets shot he recovers to get the girl. In hospital he told his wife Nancy: 'Honey, I forgot to duck.' It was a line out of an old movie, so he had no trouble getting it right again when interviewers asked him to repeat it.

Britain's Prince of Wales chose a bride. When the Three Kings of Orient visited the infant Christ in the manger it rated a few paragraphs in the Bible. For the piercingly sweet but virtually monosyllabic Lady Diana Spencer the media coverage was total and immediate, converting her from country-house obscurity to global omnipresence in twenty-four hours. The marriage was a real event, between a real heir to a real throne and a real young woman – a *really* young woman. But the wedding was a media event. Though it was immensely

An early view of Michael Jackson with a dark skin. Later he had his skin lightened, his nose bobbed and his lips remodelled – modifications which were held by his untold millions of young admirers to be without political significance, fame being a separate country where politics do not apply.

An advanced weapon system with a retarded brain, Rambo was one of the two main *personae* adopted by Sylvester Stallone. The other was Rocky, a boxer who kept coming back from defeat. Both Rambo and Rocky were bulging embodiments of the belief that in America anyone could do anything if they had sufficient determination. Stallone had excellent credentials for espousing this principle. A man who talked sideways under a brow etched with the pain of thinking, he made Charles Bronson look like Leslie Howard. But he got there. Bare-handed he climbed the sheer cliff, all the way up to the marble terrace and the divan on which Brigitte Nielsen lay outstretched.

successful, a question remained: Could an institution like royalty live by the rules of the showbusiness spectacular, especially since this one had no understudies? The Prince of Wales had fortunately been trained for the part, although judging from what happened to the previous Prince of Wales there was no guarantee that the training manual was a helpful guide. But the Princess of Wales had to do the whole thing without a single rehearsal. All the world's agony aunts combined to assure her that if she stayed natural she would be OK. She was the biggest female film star in the world but she didn't have to act. All she had to do was be. Not even the most hardened cynic was tactless enough to point out that the almost inevitable consequence of the whole world's media going bananas was that the person they went bananas about went bananas too.

This was the time when older people throughout the world became aware of Michael Jackson. Young people had been aware of him for most of their tiny lives. But their parents had never known his name except perhaps as the junior member of the Jackson Five, a Tamla Motown singing group of a previous era. Even in those days Michael stood out among his older siblings, to the extent that when the famous Tamla solo singer Diana Ross appeared on the same show she paid him the generous tribute of pushing him aside when he threatened to be too appealing.

The Jackson Four having vanished into history, the Jackson One was young Michael. One of his first incarnations was as a cartoon character, who took on independent life under the name Michael Jackson. Meanwhile the real Michael Jackson, if such a person could be said to exist, transformed himself into the tall, thin, miraculously flexible owner of a Mickey Mouse voice, the undivided loyalty of a colossal worldwide audience, and many hundreds of millions of dollars. Most of those hundreds of millions of dollars came out of parents' pockets so that their children could own the video of Jackson's song 'Thriller', in which the small child who had transformed himself into a tall child further transformed himself into a werewolf.

The teenagers who watched Michael Jackson's *Thriller* were not rebels. They were the consumer end of a global marketing operation and content to be so. Michael Jackson the organization completed the pop music industry's transformation from a Klondike concept depending on chancy hits into a steady high-volume supplier of a single artist's lifetime output. To keep his vast public plugged into the circuit, Michael Jackson the person went on transforming himself. He wore various costumes. He had plastic surgery to make his features look more Caucasian. For Americans of Afro ethnic extraction who had been fighting for acceptance of the idea that the last thing blacks should do was copy a white physical model, this looked like a setback. But a contrary school of thought held that Michael Jackson merely wanted to look like his sister, LaToya Jackson. Pursuing one or the other of these ends or perhaps both, Jackson went on having plastic surgery. He wasn't content with Caucasian features, he wanted comic-book Caucasian features. It wasn't enough to be white, he wanted to be Snow White. He was creating his own reality, and it was a fantasy.

His home in Hollywood was a castle. He had an ape for an assistant, like Tarzan. Periodically he emerged to do concerts anywhere on the planet. But his main means of communication with the outside world was through commercials for Pepsi-Cola and videos promoted through the global MTV pop music network on which every video was really a commercial for the artist. Michael Jackson was an MTV mainstay, conjuring up a united world in which all the different creeds and colours had an equal right to appear as extras while the star sang the very message he had spent millions of dollars on plastic surgery to prove that he didn't believe: 'It don't matter if you're black or white.' On any rational view, if Michael Jackson really believed what he was singing he would have left his face the way it was. But no one complained because everyone knew that the planet he inhabited wasn't really this one at all: it was fame, a parallel universe, an infantile theme park, a magic kingdom.

The soap opera *Dynasty* was another magic kingdom, a Disneyland game reserve whose leading characters were human holograms. British actress Joan Collins played the bitchy Alexis. In real life Joan Collins had been a glamour queen in British movies, suffering from the usual problem that there were no glamorous British movies. Transferred to Hollywood, she had starred in a pair of semi-porn, fully-low-budget feature films before hitting it big as Alexis, after which she never looked back, although she often looked extraordinary, especially when her shoulder-pads kept moving in one direction while she went in another.

Her ritzy British accent was regarded as defining sophistication by American TV execu-

Arnold Schwarzenegger relaxing at home with two friends. The first superstar to construct the whole of his own career from the spine outwards, Arnie had one crucial attribute he didn't need to develop on a Nautilus machine – a gift for self-mockery that got the press on his side.

A one-woman hall of fame on high heels, Madonna bolstered her own talents by transforming herself into visual echoes of every other famous woman she could think of – a stratagem which sometimes puzzled those among her young audience who could think of no famous women except her. For those whose historical perspective stretched as far back as Dusty Springfield, Madonna could offer strange, disturbing images of such distant historical figures as Marilyn Monroe, at the trifling risk of causing older spectators to be irresistibly reminded of Betty Hutton, Carmen Miranda and Little Titch.

tives who either didn't know she had been taught it at the J. Arthur Rank charm school or didn't care. Collins played Alexis as a caricature of big operatic emotions, and soon found that the media expected her own life to be like that too. Popular newspapers splashed stories about her as if she *was* Alexis, often omitting her real name. She obliged with a highly publicized emotional career featuring escorts just savvy enough to look unsurprised at being suddenly elevated above the rank of truck driver. But the fuel that kept the Joan Collins off-screen uproar going was provided by the on-screen Alexis. Effortlessly surviving the regular mass write-out at the end of each season, she set the measure for *Dynasty*'s planned absurdity. The show was a theme park. People famous in the world outside came to visit and take their turn as monsters.

Henry Kissinger made an appearance. In an earlier existence he had helped Nixon do distinguished things in foreign policy, such as burning down Cambodia. Now he was proving that his celebrity was so undeniable it could survive some self-imposed satire. If it occurred to a few people that Kissinger was already a caricature long before he even appeared in *Dynasty*, those people weren't watching. They weren't watching when ex-President Gerald Ford came on either, proving that he was big enough to take it. Only a small man bothers trying to prove that he is big enough to take it, but that objection never came up. There were no awkward questions in the magic kingdom. Fame was a resort where you could go on holiday and never come back.

Fame in America was breeding monsters, but they were bred by genetic laws which the monsters themselves understood better all the time, until finally the first fully self-constructed superstar came crunching into frame: Arnold Schwarzenegger. As mentioned earlier, he wasn't the first Austrian to be born with an urge to conquer the world. The difference was that Arnie knew how. His first move was to win the Mr Universe title. Like every previous Mr Universe, he looked like an apartment block in a posing pouch. But in the movie *Pumping Iron* he proved that he had his tongue in his cheek. The tongue in his cheek was hard to see among all his other bulges, but his trick of seeming to join in with the spectators' amazement at how he looked got him an even bigger starring role as *Conan the Barbarian*. People who read dumb books about old swords loved him.

Physically, Arnie was in the same tradition as Steve Reeves and other old-style bodybuilder B-feature stars whose acting technique had been sustained precariously by over-developed lateral muscles. But Arnie wasn't competing with them, he was up there alongside the other male stars with normal bodies. The Reaganite, Ramboesque ideal of perpetual self-reconstruction was wide open to parody. Arnie made a point of sharing the laughter. He was operating at two levels, as was his body, an organically grown original covered with an appliqué carapace of sculpted tofu. For his breakthrough film role he played himself: that is, an android, somebody someone had built – the Terminator.

And somebody *had* built him. *He* had. His brightest move of all was to let the media in on his secret. He made his career the story. He disarmingly confessed that everything was part of his plan. When he went out to perform charitable works, such as promoting the Republican Party, he cultivated his gift for making jokes about himself before anyone else did. 'Hello,' he said. 'I'm Conan the Republican.' When TV pitch-person Maria Shriver of the Kennedy clan married him, it set the seal on the deal: new fame had risen to the same status as old fame. By sheer good management, in less than ten years a bad joke had turned himself into an American national symbol, beaming his smile to the world like a male Statue of Liberty.

The small Italian female version of the large Austrian male Statue of Liberty was called Madonna. Actually she was called Madonna Louise Ciccone, but in her burning ambition for universal fame she didn't want to rule out the large section of her potential audience that might have trouble remembering more than one name. Another good reason for calling herself Madonna was that she too was engaged in the miracle of virgin birth, although in her case the miraculous human being she was giving birth to was herself.

Considering what she had to work with, she did an amazing job. She danced better than she looked and sang better than she danced and she could only just sing. But she was a world expert on twentieth-century fame. Realizing that someone famous was essentially a mystery everyone knew about, she combined rarity value with total market saturation by always making her videos more risqué than ordinary TV could carry. She earned extra publicity for being censored and so constantly added to her first fame as the biggest pop star in the world. Her concerts were just the confirmation, a source for more Madonna stories.

Even as Madonna made her initial impact she was further transforming herself. Jane Fonda had already shown the way to female bodily perfection with a video aerobics course that gave her fame as a healer to add to her fame as a political figure which had grown out of her fame as an actress. The singing actress Cher had also proved that the female body didn't have to stay the way it was, but could be refurbished, rearranged, and even torn down in some areas to be added on to somewhere else. Madonna absorbed the lessons of these pioneers and added one more example: Arnold Schwarzenegger. After a heavy course of training in the gymnasium she emerged with a new body on any part of which you could strike a match, although it looked as if it might be wise to get her permission first.

But transforming herself into a new self was only one more beginning in a career that saw every end as a new start. Madonna wasn't content to be famous for what she could do. She wanted to be famous for what other people had done as well. In rapid succession she transformed herself into all the other famous women of the century, incorporating their images into her own. She was a one-woman hall of fame, a walking museum, her only originality to borrow the originality of others. Critics who said she didn't belong with Garbo or Dietrich or Monroe were just showing their age. They were remembering the past. Madonna was taking it over on behalf of those who didn't remember it. With her, fame was the only reality. No revelation about her private life could embarrass her because she made all the revelations herself. She *had* no private life. It was all public. It went straight to video. In her film *Truth or Dare*, Warren Beatty – whose love affair with her had miraculously lasted exactly long enough to garner the publicity that helped save his tediously pretty blockbuster *Dick Tracy* from financial catastrophe – made a personal appearance to point out to her that she wasn't alive except on camera. Since Beatty had at least tried to keep himself to himself his remark had some edge, but Madonna, as if to prove his point, left it in the film. It made her more interesting, and she knew that a moment of apparent embarrassment couldn't hurt her because it was part of her story. She was so far beyond scandal that she welcomed it as light relief.

Scandal hit Ronald Reagan too, but it didn't hurt him either. News broke about a complicated illegal deal to trade arms for hostages in Iran and siphon the money to the Contras in Nicaragua. Though a cartoon character called Colonel Oliver North obligingly took the fall, many said that Ronald Reagan was the true culprit because he must have known. But they were the same people who had already made Reagan famous for not knowing anything. They couldn't have it both ways. So all Reagan had to do was look as vague as usual and he was invulnerable. Reagan's fame for vagueness worked like a suit of armour as he marched triumphantly on. The number of people who believed what he said had decreased, but his popularity had *in*creased.

Scandal in the eighties became an industry. It raked up muck about people in the past as well as in the present. All the facts came out about the late President Kennedy's fondness for attractive women. The stories might have given yet more pain to the survivors among his tragedy-stricken family, but few thought him any the less clever or charming. All the facts came out about the late Grace Kelly's fondness for attractive men. The stories might have given yet more pain to the tragedy-stricken royal family of Monaco, but few thought her any the less regal or elegant. Scandal had become part of fame's price. You couldn't even call it scandal any more – it was just coverage. A book about Frank Sinatra dwelt on his supposed Mafia connections, as if people were going to throw away their copy of *Songs for Swinging Lovers* just because Sinatra had once been seen in an Italian restaurant with a few men in silk suits who took their holidays in Sicily.

The real story was that if fame was already there, bad publicity could only feed it. In the all-star soap opera that fame had become, it was hard to change the audience's mind about any of the characters once they were established. Once they were in, they were in for life – and death. Rock Hudson, a truck driver turned film star, had been famous in the sixties as a strong, solid man of integrity who frequently made love to Doris Day. When he died of Aids in the eighties, it became blatantly clear that he had never been making love to Doris Day at all, but he was famous all over again as a strong, solid man of integrity who had bravely faced his fate. And when Liberace died from the same cause all those mothers loved him no less. The crusade against Aids needed celebrity heroes – a commodity which every good cause in the eighties went in search of and usually found.

The Live Aid concert had begun the fashion for calling in famous names to deal with world catastrophes. With thousands of people dying of hunger in Ethiopia, the Irish pop singer Bob Geldof confronted the problem by staging a worldwide satellite-linked all-star concert to raise money. His message was admirably devoid of the usual showbusiness schmaltz. 'Give us your money', he said, sometimes varying the message by saying, 'Give us your money *now*.' Though some cynics in the pop press tried to suggest that Geldof had organized the event to revitalize his flagging career, there could be no serious doubt that he was acting from the heart. He gave the project a lot more than just his time. For some of the other stars involved, however, the question was bound to arise of whether donating their time cost them as much as it cost their millions of anonymous fans to donate their money, especially when the publicity generated by the event was so great that any star who participated got a year's worth of exposure in a single night. Geldof himself was uneasily aware of this problem, but most of his fellow stars, like most of the audience, revelled in this exciting new development by which the unreal world of fame paid its tribute to the real world of suffering and reaped the reward with an inner glow to match the outer glow.

Celebrity concerts for political causes became established as a regular feature on a global scale: free Nelson Mandela, send condoms to India, save the baby seals in the rainforest. The sixties' dream of playtime politics had at last come true. Fame had developed into an ecology of its own, sustainable without cost: the world as a playground, a kindergarten. Showbiz stars were encouraged in the belief that they had a power beyond governments. Merely by doing their usual showbiz thing on a bigger stage than ever, celebrities in the West became political figures.

Political figures in the East became celebrities in the West. It started in Poland with Lech Walesa, the trade union leader who began by challenging the power of the ruling Communist Party and ended up by toppling it. He accomplished this historic feat less by persuasion than by example, bravely defying the power of the state and so inspiring the people to do the same. This was something different from fame as it had come to be understood in the West. The people's commitment to Walesa cost them something. They were risking all they had, up to and including their lives. But as Poland drew closer to the free world, Walesa couldn't prevent his Eastern fame from turning into the Western kind. The point was rubbed in when Mrs Thatcher miraculously appeared beside him to confirm his position among the world's great leaders.

The Russians didn't come to crush the Polish rebellion because they were too busy with a rebellion of their own. Theirs was led by the man in power, Mikhail Gorbachev. For a Soviet leader he looked unusually like a human being. The wary pointed out that Stalin had looked quite benevolent too. They were right to be wary, but wrong about Gorbachev. Whether or not he was making his reforms merely to retain the party's grip on power, nevertheless he made them, and the Soviet Union's previously unimaginable disintegration began.

Gorbachev had done it by the uniqueness of his personality. Again it was something different from fame in the West, and again, as the new Soviet Union drew closer to the West, Gorbachev couldn't stop his Eastern fame from turning into the Western kind. He had a Western-style glamour-puss wife, Raisa. Wives of previous Soviet leaders had looked as if they went shopping holding live chickens for barter. Raisa carried a credit card. She was enough of a Jackie O for the Western press to hail Gorby as a Kennedy-style swinging statesman. The point was rubbed in when Mrs Thatcher appeared beside him to confirm his position among the world's great leaders. Gorbachev had a fierce competitor for Mrs Thatcher's affections in Ronald Reagan, but there was only one phrase for the way the two famous men got on. They got on famously. Incredulous observers said that although their double act looked like Bud Abbott and Lou Costello the real comparison was with Francis and his Talking Mule.

Once again Reagan's fame for being clueless had misled the clever. Behind the fame was the reality, and the reality was Western society, which had left its challenger helpless to compete. The sophisticated world laughed when the suave Gorbachev and the bumbling Reagan met in Reykjavik, but it was there that Gorbachev, on behalf of the country that had led the world into revolution, finally gave up the struggle. He hadn't surrendered to Reagan. He had surrendered to reality.

Twenty years before, Soviet tanks had put a stop to reform in Czechoslovakia. This time the tanks weren't coming and Vaclav Havel was free to become what the world had never seen outside the dreams of classical philosophers: a poet king. Actually he was a playwright and had no interest in a crown, but that was just the quality which caught the world's imagination. He searched himself for the slightest sign of self-glorification. If anybody would retain his sense of proportion, he would, even when faced with overwhelming proof of his

Not long after Mikhail Gorbachev began the reforms that led to the disintegration of the Soviet Union, there were knowing voices in the West to say that he was doing it only to ensure the Communist Party's continued grip. But previous Soviet leaders had found other ways of ensuring that. Gorbachev, whatever his political motives, had an unprecedented distaste for arbitrary repression. The real puzzle was how someone recognizably human had reached the top in a system designed to eliminate any such possibility. After finally losing control of events altogether – the surest sign that he had acted from the heart – he hit the international lecture circuit.

new status. Mrs Thatcher appeared beside him to confirm his position among the world's great leaders.

Havel, though duly honoured, placed more value in the approval of Mick Jagger. For twenty long years, Czech dissidents had played their old Rolling Stones albums in secret and dreamed of better days. For them, the Stones were famous for rebellion, for liberty, for the vigour of the untamed soul. Havel invited the Stones to give a concert in Prague. Before the concert, the statue of Stalin on the hill above the city was knocked down. It was replaced with a billboard featuring Mick Jagger's tongue. The Czechs were right about the Stones. The Stones were what eastern Europe needed. But it wasn't because they were a good band. It was because they were good business. Jagger generously donated the takings of the Prague concert to Olga Havel's charity in aid of her country's myriad handicapped children neglected by the Communist regime. He could afford the gesture only because the Rolling Stones had spent the previous two decades assiduously learning to be capitalists. Jagger had unashamedly come to the point where he would make an in-house video urging sales staff to get out there and flog Stones merchandise. In the long term his revolutionary social ideal had turned out to be double-entry book-keeping.

In the Middle East the rise of Islamic fundamentalism offered powerful evidence that there could still be such a thing as a truly charismatic leader who wasn't just there for the world's entertainment and who couldn't be tamed by a visit from Mrs Thatcher or Mick Jagger. The Ayatollah Khomeini was worshipped as a god by millions of people while he was still alive. When he died, the worship turned to frenzy. Right there on television for the whole world to watch, thousands of people tried to tear him out of his coffin. What they would have done with him had they succeeded was luckily not tested. This was no Rudolph Valentino-style funeral where the famous turned up to mourn their own mortality. This was fame taken back to its origins, in religious ecstasy. We in the West looked on in disbelief at the shocking spectacle of belief.

There was a world elsewhere, and it wasn't under our control. Islamic fundamentalism condemned the writer Salman Rushdie to death for alleged blasphemy against the Prophet. Rushdie had to go into hiding in Britain, the country where he lived. Before the Fatwa was pronounced against him he was already a famous writer, but his was literary fame, fame

Salman Rushdie took what consolation he could from the courage of his publishers in bringing out a paperback edition of *The Satanic Verses* even though Islamic fundamentalists had issued death threats to prevent it. The extra fame conferred on him by the Ayatollah Khomeini, which had made him the most talked about author since Hemingway, was a privilege Rushdie would gladly have foregone.

Nobody in the West knew what an
Ayatollah was until the Ayatollah Khomeini
arrived from Paris to fill the vacuum left by
the departing Shah of Iran, whose torture
outfit Savak had at least confined its attentions
to political opponents. The Ayatollah's reign
of terror included everybody who even hinted
at a less than total commitment to Islamic
fundamentalism. The immediate result was a
large increase in the number of Islamic
fundamentalists. When the Ayatollah condemned
Salman Rushdie to death, the British government hid
Rushdie as the only possible alternative to declaring war
on Iran. The riot of grief at Khomeini's funeral proved
either that he had been really popular all along or else that
the next Ayatollah was watching the screen on
the lookout for insufficient enthusiasm.

among the discerning. After the Fatwa he became the most famous writer since Hemingway but it wasn't his fame, it was another kind, one he would dearly have liked to be without. His name was a household word in millions of houses that once didn't count but now did.

In Iraq, Saddam Hussein was a leader who used all the personality cult trappings of the old-style Marxist regimes but seemed to need little of the coercive apparatus because the people were crazy about him, no matter how crazy he might be himself. When he invaded Kuwait, the West sent General Stormin' Norman Schwarzkopf to stop him. The Gulf War was a media event and Stormin' Norman was dream casting for the lead, having apparently modelled his flamboyant persona on John Wayne, Rambo, Terminator II, Lethal Weapon III, Superman IV and Indiana Jones in the Temple of Doom. Wiseacres in the West found it easier to make jokes about him than to condemn Saddam. The marketable glamour of the West – that we knew about. We knew it had a bogus element built in. Our clumsy heroes were in on the gag. Real evil was too authentic, too vivid a reminder that even if the Cold War had been called off there were all these awkward little hot wars waiting to ensure that history wasn't over, it was just warming up.

For seventy years, Lenin's fame had been the wedge that kept the world divided. If his image now suddenly crumbled, it wasn't because he had become symbolic. It was because for a long time symbolic had been all he was. There was nothing behind him. The power and the will to compel the people to believe in what he represented were all gone. His fame was hollow.

In the West, fame looked hollow too, but we had the advantage of knowing that it was bound to look that way. More than ninety years of continuous development of the mechanisms of publicity had given us the twenty-four-hour fame spectacular. It was self-sustaining. The Japanese bought Hollywood, but the show went on just as before. It didn't even need the American economy any more because it was part of the world economy. It was the most glamorous by-product of the new global information society, and we had come to understand it because the information came with it.

It was an international entertainment complex of electronic theme parks all staffed by people who looked like cartoons. The beautiful people were like cartoons of beautiful people. Julia Roberts had a cartoon mouth. Tom Cruise had cartoon teeth. Harrison Ford

Warren Beatty got closer than any other famous man to using the press without it using him. Having managed to erect promiscuity to the status of a principle, he was hard to hurt with scandal. A carefully calculated reputation for almost total inarticulacy meant that the few tormented phrases he did occasionally utter were greeted by reporters as an exclusive interview. Perhaps his greatest public relations coup was to fall in love with Madonna for exactly as long as it took the resulting press coverage to help *Dick Tracy* break even.

had a cartoon jaw. Mel Gibson had cartoon hair. The beautiful people fell in love with each other in various combinations. John loved Tatum. Tatum's father Ryan loved Farrah. Woody loved Diane. Diane loved Warren. Warren loved Madonna for five minutes.

The rich people were like cartoons of rich people. Donald Trump looked as if he had been drawn by Garry Trudeau in a fit of anger. He made money, and made more money writing a book about how he made it. Ivana Trump had herself rebuilt to look like the kind of bimbo he was dumb enough to leave her for. She made money from the divorce, and made more money writing a book about how her husband lost money. Reality didn't enter the equation at any point.

Fame was a sham, but it was *our* sham. It was a sham we couldn't do without, a show we had to see. The best performers were the ones born for nothing else. Elizabeth Taylor went on and on giving her heart to progressively more obscure men, attracting more publicity for the wedding the more she kept the press at bay, until finally she married a construction worker and caused a world media sensation by shutting the reporters out entirely, so that they had to hang in the sky above like starving vultures. She had completed the process of transforming herself from a screen star who actually did something into a stage presence who simply was. She had become an essence. She had become a fragrance. She was Michael Jackson's mother. She was the Fairy Godmother.

When Ronald Reagan came into office his detractors had to admit that he had charm. By the time he left it, his supporters could defend his conduct only by insisting that he had lost his memory. He had also lost most of America's money. Yet he left the show just as popular as when he joined it, and fixed it for his understudy, George Bush, to take over the role. It looked as if fame had taken over from the facts.

It looked as if fame could conquer death. As the technology advanced to the stage where it could create any illusion, the whole twentieth century went on to video and the fast forward looked like a rewind. Famous people from then – Humphrey Bogart, Louis Armstrong – started to show up in commercials made now. It was a sort of eternal life, except it was for the image and not the soul. If the real person might have objected, the real person wasn't here. It looked as if the spectacle had wiped out the reality. But reality was still there. Fame could distort it but not destroy it. It did its own destroying. When one of Marlon Brando's children went on trial for murder, the star had to come out of his Pacific island fortress and do what he had never had to do before: plead with the press. He begged them not to take it out on his children. He was too late. His fame had already taken it out on his children. Woody Allen, the model of self-questioning sanity, the famous man who had come nearest to reaping all the benefits of fame while staving off its drawbacks, suddenly found himself accused of child molestation by his *de facto* wife, thought to defend himself by proclaiming his sincere love for her daughter, and thus inadvertently revealed to an astonished world that at some point he had fallen prey to a delusion – that he was a private citizen of Sweden.

The famous people were living human beings. Not even showbusiness could conceal that fact, and outside showbusiness it showed up with cruel clarity. Amateur actors who forgot their lines were savagely punished when they found that all the attention could not be switched off. The Royal Family was an institution the British had that the Americans hadn't. But the Royal Family had let publicity into the Palace under the impression that it was the same as daylight, and the result was all the razzle-dazzle of the international media circus with none of the capacity to engineer the outcome. There was no way back to secrecy. There was nowhere to run. If the Prince of Wales had gone to the moon there would have been reporters waiting. If the Princess of Wales had gone to a nunnery the Mother Superior would have been Oprah Winfrey. The two most privileged people in the world were human sacrifices, like those randomly chosen youngsters the Aztecs would treat as royalty for a few nights, and then cut out their hearts. Their best hope was that we would understand.

And by and large we did. Ninety years before, it would have been more of a mystery. But with only a few years of the twentieth century left to run, the workings of fame had become so immense, so dazzling and so noisy that they stood revealed for all to see. Fame is a luminous and therefore limited version of the world, but without it we couldn't cope with the world's complexity. We all need a map, and all maps are drastic simplifications. To quarrel with them on that account is pointless. What we should be concerned with is whether the map is a good one and leads to the treasure, which is the reasonable truth.

Ninety-nine per cent of all the scientists who have ever lived have been alive in the twentieth century. We can't remember them all, but we all need to know the name of at

As much marvellous man as you can get in one piece, Luciano Pavarotti, the most famous tenor since Caruso, became the one and only operatic voice most people had ever heard when he sang the Puccini aria *Nessun' dorma* as the official anthem of the soccer World Cup in Rome in 1990. Though fond of his stellar privileges, he remained unspoiled by his enormous fame, guarded against *folie de grandeur* by the conviction that his voice was a gift from God.

Despite rumours, Mother Teresa was never in search of a recording contract.

least one person who can comprehend what we can't. It might as well be Einstein, who really did have the all-embracing, generous world view to match his creative brilliance. We all need to know the name of at least one person who can sing the way we can't. It might as well be Pavarotti, who really does sing for the love of life. We all need to know the name of at least one person who is good the way we aren't. It might as well be Mother Teresa, who really *isn't* after that recording contract. It does us no harm that Hitler is our ready symbol of a man more evil than we are, Lindbergh of a man more brave, the young Marlon Brando of a man more beautiful. It does us good. The famous help us live. What they do, they do for us. Fame is what we do to them. We turn them into characters and put them in a show, a modern version of the passion play. The ones we respect burn like angels. The ones who ask for worship burn like witches. Fame, like happiness, ruins anyone who pursues it for its own sake, and exalts only those who have proper work to do.

Those who are famous have their importance only to the extent that they help give meaning to the lives of those who aren't. Ordinary life isn't just the hardest kind to lead, it's the best, and the famous people we like the most seem to tell us that by their way of staying human, as if there were a fallible, frail human being behind the glory – which there always is.

INDEX

Picture Credits

BBC Books would like to thank the following for providing photographs and for permission to reproduce copyright material.

© Advertising Archive 119; Associated Press 206, 216, 224; Allsport/Steve Powell 213 (right); Barnaby's Picture Library 41, 59, 118, 142; Bridgeman Art Library 22; British Film Institute 47, 106 (lower) Turner Entertainment; British Museum 18; Camera Press 50 (left), 64 & 99 (Cecil Beaton), 129, 132, 147 (Karsh), 151, 153, 165 (Karsh), 182–3, 203 (left), 227 (Patrick Demarchelier), 230; E.T. Archive 23; Fotos International 207 (top right); Tim Graham 226; Ronald Grant Archive 73, 82, 106 (top) Turner Entertainment, 114 (top), 123, 154, 167 / 20th Century Fox, 215; Hulton Deutsch Collection 25–34, 63, 66, 76, 85, 103–5, 108, 122, 126, 187, 195, 220; Imperial War Museum 78, 112–13, 114 (lower); Kobal Collection 43, 69, 70, 90, 91, 198 (right), 202, 203 (right); Magnum 139 (Eve Arnold), 145 (Robert Capa), 148 (Burt Glinn), 179 (Cornell Capa), 198 (left), 244 (David Hurn) 245, 250; NASA 191; Pictorial Press 44, 60, 135, 138, 157, 203 (top), 207 (lower right), 211 (top) 231, 234; Popperfoto 39, 50 (right), 53–6, 79, 96, 168, 186, 190, 199, 211 (lower); Redferns 177 (Val Wilmer); Rex Features 86, 158, 159, 172, 174, 207 (left); 235, 247, 251; Scott Polar Research Institute 36 (left); Frank Spooner/Gamma 213 (left) 242; Springer/Bettmann Film Archive 95; Syndication International 36 (right).